CW01594493

The Litt
Workbench 1.3
Book

Mark Smiddy

Kuma Computers Ltd.

Other Titles in the Kuma Range:

Commodore Amiga

Intuition A Practical Programmers Guide by Mike Nelson	07457 0143 4
Program Design Techniques for the Amiga by Paul Overaa	07457 0032 2
The Little Red Workbench 1.3 Book by Mark Smiddy	07457 0048 9
The Little Blue Workbench 2 Book by Mark Smiddy	07457 0055 1

IBM PC & Compatible Micros

Desktop Publishing Sourcebook - Fonts & Clip Art for the PC by Jami L Borman	07457 0030 6
PageMaker 4.0 for Windows by William B. Sanders	07457 0031 4
ZBasic Quick Reference Guide for PC & Mac by John Sumner	07457 0140 X
The Windows Guide Book by Gill & Vic Gerhardi & Andy Berry	07457 0041 1
The Timeworks Guide by Terry Freedman	07457 0147 7
The DR DOS 6 Quick Start Guide by John Sumner	07457 0038 1
Illustrated DR DOS 6 - The First 20 Hours by John Sumner	07457 0044 6

Apple Macintosh

Desktop Publishing Sourcebook - Fonts & Clip Art for the Mac by Jami L Borman	07457 0050 0
ZBasic Quick Reference Guide for PC & Mac by John Sumner	07457 0140 X
Superpaint - Complete User Guide by Gia Rozells	07457 0051 9
The Quark Book by Rod Lawton & Isaac Davis	07457 0052 7

Psion Organiser

Psion Organiser Deciphered by Gill Gerhardi, Vic Gerhardi & Andy Berry	07457 0139 6
Using & Programming the Psion Organiser by Mike Shaw	07457 0134 5
File Handling on the Psion Organiser by Mike Shaw	07457 0135 3
Machine Code Programming on the Psion Organiser 2nd Ed. by Bill Aitken	07457 0138 8
Psion Organiser Communications Handbook by Gill & Vic Gerhardi & Andy Berry	07457 0154 X
Structured Programming in OPL by Bill Aitken	07457 0033 0

Cambridge Z88

Z88 Magic by Gill Gerhardi, Vic Gerhardi & Andy Berry	07457 0137 X

Games Consoles

Sega Megadrive Secrets by Rusel deMaria	07457 0037 3
Sega Megadrive Secrets Volume 2 by Rusel deMaria	07457 0043 8

Psion Series 3

First Steps in Programming the Psion Series 3 by Mike Shaw	07457 0145 0
Introduction to Using the Psion Series 3 by Rod Lawton	07457 0146 9
Serious Programming on the Psion Series 3 by Bill Aitken	07457 0035 7

Atari ST

Atari ST Explored 2nd Ed. by John Braga & Malcolm McMahon	07457 0141 8
Program Design Techniques for the Atari ST by Paul Overaa	07457 0029 2
Programming by Example - ST Basic by Dr. Graham McMaster	07457 0143 4
Desk Top Publishing With Calamus by Terry Freedman	07457 0159 0
The Timeworks Guide by Terry Freedman	07457 0147 7

The Little Red Workbench 1.3 Book

"Now located at the Earl's Court in London, the World of Commodore Show splits into two halves: the mail-order dealers and the more serious companies. It's the place to see the people that make the world of Amiga tick, point fingers, take pictures, and perhaps throw them a few nuts. It is also the best place to go if you need straight talking, impartial advice from the experts."

© Mark Smiddy 1990-1991

ISBN: 07457 0049 0

First printing December 1991

Edited by Don Smiddy

Published by Kuma Computers Ltd. 12 Horseshoe Park, Pangbourne, Berks. RG8 7JW

Set in Century Schoolbook, Helvetica, and Courier by the author

Amiga is a registered trademark of Commodore-Amiga, Inc.

Amiga A500, Amiga A500 Plus, Amiga A1500, Amiga A2000, AmigaDOS, Amiga Workbench and Amiga Kickstart and trademarks of Commodore- Amiga Inc. Commodore, the Commodore logo and CBM are trademarks of Commodore Electronics, Ltd.

All other trademarks used or otherwise implied are acknowledged.

Disclaimer: While every effort has been made to ensure the accuracy of the text contained herein, and any programs or software mentioned directly or by implication, the publisher and author cannot accept any responsibility for any consequential loss or damage, however caused, arising as a result of using the information presented here.

This book is sold subject to standard conditions of sale: namely that it not be lent, sold hired or otherwise disposed of in any form or binding than that which it had at the time of original sale without the publisher's prior written consent.

Printed by Antony Rowe Ltd, Chippenham, Wiltshire

The Little Red Workbench 1.3 Book

Mark Smiddy

Kuma Computers Ltd.

About the Author

Mark Smiddy started a career in computers selling Dragon 32s because they had a proper keyboard. After that brief excursion into the retail trade he became a programmer, but quickly realised that few Acorn BBC owner's actually played games and became a freelance computer journalist because there was precious little left that suited his unusual lifestyle.

Mark lives in the one remaining rural part of ancient Cleveland, near enough to the North Sea to see it – but not go paddling at lunchtime. He is 5'11" tall, claims to be in his late 20's and grows bonsai trees for a hobby because they don't answer back and never shed hairs on the sofa.

For the really interested, he is Consultant Editor to Amiga Shopper, contributes to Amiga Format [when the Editor lets him] and is a former Editorial Coordinator of Amiga User International.

Also by Mark Smiddy

Mastering AmigaDOS 2 Volume 1 [w. Bruce Smith]

Mastering AmigaDOS 2 Volume 2

both published by Bruce Smith Books

Contents

Introduction

This is a book for everyone.

The Amiga is a powerful yet much misunderstood machine and Workbench is part of the key to harnessing that power. However, the power of Workbench — and its brother-in-arms, AmigaDOS — is also its downfall and something that many beginners, like you perhaps, will find a little awe inspiring at first.

As you embark of this trek into the unknown, never forget, even the wise man was a toddler once – taking those first tentative steps on the journey of experiment towards the temple of wisdom. But enough waxing of the lyrical — any more and I'll run out of polish.

> **"Experts are not born.**
>
> **They are hewn from the bedrock of endeavour,**
>
> **and the granite of experience."**

Brace yourself; it's time for a little home truth. This book was not typeset on an Amiga A500. Other than testing the tutorials and doing screenshots I only used the Amiga for playing the odd game (HiSoft's ProFlight mostly). It's sad to reflect this book was typeset using Microsoft Word 4 on a Apple Macintosh and output on a GCC LED page printer.

Why? Because as yet, Amiga software (in this particular area) just doesn't come up to scratch. I have no doubt it would have been possible to get the same output quality (one 300 DPI optical printer is pretty much the same as the next) but I wouldn't have trusted this amount of text to what's available now. (Mind you, the word processing software alone cost the best part of £300)

Little Red Workbench Book a complete reference to get you started with the Amiga. If, after reading this book you understand just 20 per cent more of this fascinating machine, its world and people that live in it, this book will have done its job.

The tutorials within these pages are self-contained but to get the best out of them you are advised to take each one a step at a time. AmigaDOS for instance is a very complex and confusing thing to work with; it still makes my eyes glaze over sometimes. Therefore, don't go diving head first into a Shell until you at least know the rudiments of what is going on.

Before I sign off, a few words of the people behind this book. Damien Noonan created the seed; my Parents Don and Olwyn nurtured it; and Jon Day picked the fruit. Dicon Peeke designed the original cover, Pat Winstanley and Mike Nelson provided moral support. Oh yeah, This one's for you Michelle—you earned it.

Enough waffle! The Amiga's a fun machine — enjoy it.

Mark Smiddy

November 1991

Welcome

> *In the beginning Amiga created the machine.*
>
> *And it was good.*
>
> *And Amiga said unto the machine, "go out into the world machine and blow their minds with superlative graphics and amazing stereo sound."*
>
> *And the user did install software.*
>
> *But it was not good.*
>
> *And thus the guru spake unto the user in humbling tones.*
>
> *And the guru said, "81000009".*

It's fair to say, every seasoned Amiga owner, will at some time have had an experience of the Guru. The machine freezes, the screen drops by about an inch and a hideous red flashing box framed against a black background appears bearing the message "Guru Meditation" and some rather confusing numbers. It does little for the heart rate, less for the stress level, and tends to make you think, what did I do wrong? Let's get something straight. You did nothing wrong — the program did.

People are frightened by computers — and the Amiga's guru system does little to ease this fear. Never get the idea the computer is in control, YOU are. Overcoming this simple (natural) fear is the first and most important step you will take on the road to understanding the machine. Strangely enough, this fear seems to resurface every time we change to a new, more powerful micro. Introduced to the Amiga, the seasoned Spectrum, C64 or BBC user, finds him or herself thrust into a world of complexities they were previously unaware of — not least a fully multi-tasking, WIMP environment. Curiously, this is where the "real" beginner has the advantage over the old hacks, because they are devoid of any preconceived ideals.

Avoiding Disaster

At this point, it has to be assumed you have at least managed to put all the bits together. Now you're ready and itching to start the machine — wait — there are several rules which must be followed before proceeding. Amigas, like most modern computers, are inert. They derive all their energy from mains electricity. Unlike humans, they do not require additional carbohydrates, air or even water so:

✗ Never eat or drink near one. Tea; and coffee are bad enough, but fizzy drinks spell a cocktail of disasters. Because of the huge sugar content, a splash of lemonade, coke, or even still-orange will jam a keyswitch as fast as epoxy resin and it's just as hard to remove. Worse, if these materials get onto the PCB they can eat through the copper tracks and short circuit components. Like a cancer, these maladies take time to become noticeable — even a small spill could cause trouble for months.

✗ Smoking should be avoided too (at the risk of a broadside from ASH) in practice the only damage it can do to a robust modern micro like the Amiga is indirect — like singeing the plastic case! The 3.5" micro floppy disks used by the Amiga are almost impervious to smoke and other foreign particles — apart from prying fingers and liquids.

✗ The machine has very few moving parts — and all the moving parts are self-lubricating. This means you *must not* go fiddling with a can of WD- 40 or 3-In-1. Amiga disk drives are quite noisy — this is normal.

✗ Lastly, this warning applies to everyone, especially to users upgrading from machines such as Spectrums, BBCs and C64s. If you have to reset the machine use the CTRL-Amiga-Amiga sequence described in the manual. Do NOT switch it off and on again unless you have to. If you must do it this way, leave the machine switched OFF for AT LEAST 10 seconds before switching on again. This point cannot be stressed strongly enough.

Getting Going

You will need

☞ Your Amiga system, plugged in and ready to switch on.

☞ A disk marked Workbench

☞ At least one blank disk

When you switch on (and tune the TV channel if necessary) you'll get a picture of a hand holding a big blue thing carrying the words "Amiga Workbench". The picture is upside down — but don't worry, that's a historical hangover to tell you how to put a disk in. Below this is a number — either 1.2 or 1.3. Make a note of it, it's the version number of the Kickstart installed in your machine and it can be important when software refuses to load — more on that later. Most new machines should display version 1.3, whereas second hand ones will be 1.2 — at this stage the difference is immaterial.

A1000 users will need to boot (insert) a Kickstart disk first. On any machine, if the power light comes on but, after a few seconds, the display is showing red, yellow, green, or blue without the usual "hand and disk" picture — — switch off and check the problem solving guide in Appendix F.

Now, insert a *blank* disk in the internal drive and watch carefully. You should notice that the hand-disk icon vanishes for a short time then comes back again. (If your machine has a hard disk — say an A590 — and a 1.3 Kickstart, there's a good chance none of this happened and you're now staring at the Workbench screen.

Why? The Amiga is intelligent enough to recognise you have inserted a disk so it attempts to boot from it. However, since this was a blank disk it repeats the question for a Workbench disk. Workbench disks are specially prepared disks — because it's safer to only boot from a disk that's been specially prepared. This way you don't go around accidentally trying to boot a data disk. This exercise has been about finding out what happens when you make a mistake. This way, you'll soon learn to recognise what the Amiga is trying to tell you.

Now you're itching to get started, remove the blank disk. But before inserting the Workbench disk, make a note of the version number: 1.2, 1.3 or 1.3.2. When you've done that, insert the disk and wait for the Workbench screen to appear.

Welcome to Workbench

This is Workbench — one of the most friendly GUIs (Graphical User Interfaces) around. Let's see how good it is. First, remove the Workbench disk from your internal drive — this is also called DF0: or Unit 0.

Now, move the pointer over the small picture marked Workbench 1.x and press the left mouse button twice in quick succession. This operation is called a double-click and is used to "open" a disk. Opening a disk, is rather like opening a drawer to find out what's inside. However, since you've just removed the disk from the drive, the Amiga brings up a message box (called a requester) asking you to replace the correct disk (called a volume) in any drive.

Now position the pointer over the box marked "Cancel" and press the left mouse button once. This is called a *click* and clicking a button in this way is called *selecting a gadget*. Here, the Cancel box is the gadget. The screen will flash briefly and a message will appear at the the top of the screen stating, "This drawer cannot be opened."

Go back over the last few steps and try to "open" the Workbench 1.2/3 disk once more. When the requester appears, pop the Workbench 1.2/3 disk back in the drive and WAIT. After a couple of seconds the requester vanishes (as if by magic) and a new *window* appears showing the contents of the disk. Notice, there's usually no need for you to tell the Amiga you have inserted a disk, it can work that out for itself.

Lesson 1
Making A Backup

You will need:

☞ Your Workbench disk

☞ Two blank, 3.5" micro-floppy disks.

The next job, especially if you're new to the machine, is to make a two copies of the Workbench disk. This is vital — if the original becomes faulty the machine will be rendered totally useless, except for playing games. What happens next is very dependent on which version of Workbench you have — because there's a curious bug in the Workbench 1.3.2 version of the command used to copy an entire disk.

Diskcopy for 1.2 and 1.3

This job, like most on the Amiga is much simpler if you have more than one drive. For the purposes of this exercise, I'll assume you only have one drive.

1. Insert the Workbench 1.2/3 disk in DF0: — the internal drive

2. Click once on the disk's icon — it will change colour slightly to confirm this

3. Press and hold the *right* mouse button. The white bar at the top of the screen will now show:

```
Workbench Disk Special:
```

4. Move the pointer to the word Workbench and a small "menu" will appear with the following options: Open, Close, Duplicate, Rename, Info, Discard. By moving the pointer to each word in turn, you'll see a bar appear. Notice some of the choices cannot be selected, this is for safety. (If you cannot select any of the options, go back to the Workbench disk icon and click it again.) When the bar is over the word Duplicate, release the button and a requester will appear asking you to insert the source disk in drive DF0: will appear.
5. Click on the gadget marked ";Continue". A small window will appear showing the progress of the diskcopy operation and after a short while another requester will appear. Elsewhere on the Workbench, the disk icon will change to say "DF0:Busy"
6. Now, remove the Workbench disk from the drive, insert one of the blank disks you have to hand, and select the gadget marked continue.
7. Repeat the last two steps until the message "Diskcopy finished" appears.
8. After a few seconds the message window will disappear and you will now have another disk icon marked "Copy of Workbench1.x"

9. Click once on the disk icon marked "Copy of Workbench". Now press and hold the right mouse button and move the pointer to the Workbench menu (as before) but this time select "Rename". A small box will appear containing the name of the disk — this is called a Text Gadget.

10. Point at the letter "C" in Copy and press the left mouse button. Now press the key marked "Del" a few times until the words "Copy of" have been removed. Finally press either the key marked "Enter" or the Return key — it's marked with a ↲.

11. Repeat the entire operation for the second blank disk. Mark it "Copy of Workbench" (plus the date) them put it and the original in a *safe* place. Next time you are asked for Workbench, use one of the copies — never the original.

Diskcopy for 1.3.2

You will need

☞ Your Workbench disk

☞ Two blank, 3.5" micro-floppy disks.

This version of Workbench saw an unforeseen bug creep into the Diskcopy command so it only works from the Shell.

1. As described above, insert the Workbench 1.3.2 disk into drive df0: and open it by double clicking on its icon.

2. Look for an icon marked "Shell" and open in the same way as you opened disk. Shell is a tricky subject which I'll cover in a little more depth later on. For now though, just follow the instructions. At the end of each line press the key marked "↵" or "Enter" on your keyboard. If you're not sure which one this is, consult the manual supplied with the machine.

3. When the Shell is started it opens a window and displays a "prompt" which looks something like this:

```
1.SYS>.
```

This is Shell's way of telling you it's ready to accept commands which you must type from the keyboard. The following instructions mirror a typical session. What you see is what you enter. Text in **bold like this** is what AmigaDOS (the Shell will display. At the end of each line press the Return key (↵).

```
DISKCOPY DF0: to DF0: NAME "Workbench1.3"
Place SOURCE disk (FROM disk) in drive DF0:
Press RETURN to continue
```

4. Now press Return and to get the following:

```
Reading XX, XX to go
Place DESTINATION disk (TO disk) in drive DF0:
Press RETURN to continue
```

5. Pop the disk you are copying **to** in the internal drive and press Return again.Shell replies;

```
Writing XX, XX to go
```

6. You may have to change disks several times during this operation. It depends on how much memory is fitted to the machine. Make sure you put the correct disk in each time though! When the counter reaches 79 the shell replies:

```
Writing 79, 00 to go
Diskcopy finished
```

7. Repeat these steps for the second disk. At the prompt type:

```
ENDCLI
```

The Shell window will go away. Now mark both disks "Copy of Workbench" plus the date and put the original and one of the copies away in a safe place. Next time you are asked for Workbench, use one of the copies — never the original.

HouseKeeping

Housekeeping is all about keeping your disks in good order. For instance, making sure every time you open a disk the icons appear in an orderly way; getting rid of old files — that sort of thing. First of all though, you need to know how to make a new drawer to store things in.

Lesson 2
Making a New Drawer

You will need

☞ Your Workbench disk

Drawers are the places we use to keep things in. Utilities like NotePad and Clock live in the Utilities drawer; the Preferences live in the Prefs drawer and so on. It's a convenient way of organising things and makes life a lot easier in the long term — provided you put everything away in the correct place. For instance, you don't keep trousers in the sock drawer but you might keep your *drawers* in there. In this lesson, we'll create a new drawer for extra bits and pieces.

1. Open the Workbench disk

2. Click on the Empty drawer. (Note how the icon changes to a picture of an open drawer? That means it's selected.)

3. Now select Duplicate from the Workbench menu. After a short time, a new drawer will appear bearing the name “Copy of Empty”.
4. Click on the new drawer to select it.
5. Select Rename from the Workbench menu and a text gadget will appear and wait for you to enter the new name. You can do this by deleting the old name just as if you were renaming a disk, but this time we’ll use a different method. Hold down the right-Amiga key (A) and press X.. This deletes the contents of the text gadget.
6. Enter a new name — let’s call this new drawer, Extras — and press Return.

Lesson 3
Snapshotting an icon

You will need

☞ Your Workbench disk

Snapshot is a frequently misunderstood feature of Workbench. Its main function is to fix icons at a specific location in a window. When you copy an icon using Workbench, it usually adopts its original position relative to its old window — which inevitably looks messy.

You can move the icon somewhere else in the window — but when you close and re-open it, the icon is back where it started. The situation gets even worse when something creates a new drawer — because the new icon gets covered by the old one. For this example, I will use the Extras drawer just created — the same technique applies to all icons however.

1. Open the Workbench disk by double-clicking its icon.
2. Select the Extras drawer and move (drag) it to a free part of the disk. (Note: you may have to re-size the window to do this.)
3. Press and hold the right mouse button.
4. Go to the Special menu and move the pointer down so that the "Snapshot" option is highlighted.
5. Release the right mouse button. This operation will "fix" the Extras drawer in place.

Lesson 4
Changing a Drawer's Contents

You will need

☞ Your Workbench disk

There are times when you'll want to move icons to different parts of the disk. For example, you may want to move some documents into a new drawer you've created specifically for them.

1. Open the Workbench disk.
2. Open the Utilities and Extras Drawers.
3. Click once in the Workbench screen (to ensure the drawers are not selected).

4. Hold either Shift key.
5. Select the Clock icon.
6. Select the Calculator icon.
7. Drag the Calculator icon over the Extras drawer's window — notice how the Clock comes with it.
8. When the pointer is over the Extras drawer, release the mouse button and drop both icons back in. Release the shift key now. Note: it is only necessary to position the pointer over the drawer when copying/moving multiple objects. All the selected objects will move. When using this technique, be careful not to select more objects than you intend.
9. Now follow steps 3 to 8 and put the icons back where they should be.

Lesson 5
Snapshotting Several Icons

You will need

☞ Your Workbench disk

At some point you might want to completely reorganise the visual layout of a disk. It may be you have discarded some files, added others, or just moved some things around. A typical case would be where you have moved some icons into another drawer or created a new drawer from scratch. Icons could have come from elsewhere on the same disk or, more often, from a completely different disk.

1. Drag Clock, NotePad and Calculator (from Utilities) into the Extras drawer.
2. Move the icons around until you are happy with the layout.
3. Hold either of the two Shift keys down.
4. Point and click (left button) on each icon in the Extras drawer in turn. (You should notice the image changes slightly to indicate selection.) Do this slowly or you might accidentally start one of the programs.
5. Hold the left button down over one of your icons and move the mouse a little. Notice how all the selected icons move at once? This is a quick way to make sure you have selected the right ones.
6. Release the Shift key.
7. Press the right mouse button and select Snapshot from the special menu as described above. The disk light will come on for a short time while Workbench updates the dot-info files. Your Workbench disk must be write-enabled for this to work.

Lesson 6
Using Trashcan

You will have realised by now, the Workbench disk is just about full to overflowing; and some of the programs on there are superfluous to your daily requirements. Removing the excess is something you will need to do from time to time. Workbench provides two methods for clearing files — the aptly named Trashcan and the Discard function. These work slightly differently, so let's examine them one at a time:

The Trashcan is actually a special Drawer. Think of the Workbench disk as being your office — where the drawers belong to various filing cabinets. When you are finished with something, you throw it in the waste paper basket — the trashcan. You can always retrieve things from the bin until someone empties it. Any objects placed in the bin stay in the office *until* someone empties it. In effect, although some of the clutter is removed, the same amount of space is still used up. The same thing happens on a Workbench disk. When you move things to the trash, they still take up the same amount of space on the disk.

1. Open the Utilities drawer.

2. Drag the InstallPrinter icon to the RAM Disk icon.

3. Open the RAM disk and drag the InstallPrinter icon over the the Trashcan and release the button. Notice that InstallPrinter still exists in RAM Disk and Utilities.

4. Select Trashcan — notice how the image changes.

5. Open the Trashcan — you should see InstallPrinter.

6. Select "Empty Trash" from the Disk menu and you will see InstallPrinter vanish.

As this example proves, Trashcan is a bit of a white elephant. In this case I just duplicated an icon in the trash to show what happens. Normally if you move something directly to the trash, then empty the bin, it's gone for good!

Lesson 7
Using Discard

You will need

☞ Your Workbench disk

Getting rid of unwanted files is more usefully performed by Discard. This example assumes you have followed the instructions above:

1. Open the RAM Disk.
2. Select the InstallPrinter icon.
3. Select "Discard" from the "Workbench" menu.
4. A requester will appear asking if that's really what you want to do — once an item has been discarded from a disk it cannot be recovered.
5. Click "ok to discard".
6. InstallPrinter will disappear from the RAM Disk. This is just like emptying the Trashcan. Once something has been deleted, you can not get it back!

Lesson 8
Snapshotting a Drawer

You will need

☞ Your Workbench disk

A less well known feature of Snapshot is its ability to memorise the size and location of Workbench drawer windows when they are opened. This can come in very useful because it allows you to have several drawers at once without lots of overlap. Understanding this is the key to understanding how the Snapshot facility works. A well-organised Workbench is a largely personal preference — but here's how to do it.

1. Open the drawer you want to work with.

2. Adjust the size and position of the drawer.

3. Select the drawer's icon. (It may already be selected — but it won't hurt to check.) If you can't see the drawer, just push any other windows out of the way.

4. Select Snapshot from the Special menu. You can Snapshot ANY icon on the Workbench except the RAM Disk. And that includes the Workbench disk itself.

Lesson 9
Cleaning Up After Yourself

The Clean Up option found under Workbench's Special menu is used to automatically arrange icons into a more organised manner. The problem is, Clean Up does not work quite as you might expect — that is: you cannot just select a number of icons (as you would for a Snapshot) and perform a Clean Up on them. As it turns out, Clean Up is easier to operate than Snapshot.

You will need

☞ Your Workbench disk

Try the following steps — reading them before you begin:

1. Boot the Workbench disk.
2. Open the Utilities drawer.
3. Click and hold on the drawer's sizer gadget and drag it until you can see most of the icons. As you do this, you will notice the window does not refresh (redraw itself) while you are dragging. In view of this, you may have to stop dragging (release the button) to discover if all the icons are visible.
4. Drag a few of the icons around. Make a mess, go on — it doesn't matter. Note: do not try this willy-nilly example with any drawers or you might find some of your icons disappear into the inner reaches of the directory hierarchy and from then on who knows where...
5. Now select Clean Up from the Special menu.
6. I deliberately chucked a spanner in there to make sure you are paying attention. You will not be able to

select Clean Up because the option is *shadowed.* — that is, not available.

7. Select the Utilities drawer in the Workbench window.

8. Go to the Special menu, and, surprise, Clean Up is now available. Select the option and watch those icons fly. In order to fix the icons in their new positions you now have to go round and snapshot them all. This clash of techniques between Snapshot and Clean Up has been rectified in Workbench 2, which is yet another reason for upgrading.

Two Golden Rules

☞ Snapshot only works on selected icons

☞ Clean Up operates on disks and drawers — but the relevant icon must be opened *and* selected before it will work.

Lesson 10
If Snapshot, Empty Trash and Discard fail

You will need

☞ Your Workbench disk

One of the most unforgiving features of Workbench is the way it handles unexpected AmigaDOS errors. A typical case is one where you attempt to snapshot an icon which has been write-protected. In this instance, Workbench responds: "Error while writing nnnn: 222" where "nnnn" is the name of the icon involved. This problem is a nuisance but it can easily be got round by clearing the not-deleteable flag in the icon's info box. Much the same rules apply to Empty Trash and Discard from the Workbench menu. Here is how to fix this:

1. Select the offending icon.
2. Select Info from the Workbench menu.
3. Click on the not-deleteable flag box.
4. Select save to re-configure the icon
5. Attempt the Snapshot, Discard or Empty Trash operation again.
6. Repeat steps**1...5** as often as required.

Lesson 11
Snapshot — the untold story

This is not so much a lesson — as one of those tips you only hear about whispered in dark recesses of local pubs sometime after the last bell has gone. It may not seem much use at the moment, but there may come a time when you'll find this tip invaluable.

When you open a drawer, Workbench memorises all the icons' images — as well as all the other relevant information. This means if you happen to be working in the Shell and accidentally erased all the icon (dot-info) files, all you have to do is select all the icons and Snapshot them back. Easy huh? This only works while the window is open of course — but it is worth knowing; if only for the one-upmanship — because very few "experts" know this!

Summary

By now you should be a little more familiar with what goes on inside your machine. So from now on I'll assume you understand what is meant by terms like Open, Select and so on. Here is a quick resume:

Click	Press the left mouse button once.
Drag	Select an icon and move the mouse while holding the left mouse button.
Double-click	Press the left mouse button twice in quick succession.
Icon	Picture representing a Tool or Project.
Select	Click on an icon OR release the right mouse button on a menu option.

<table>
<tr><th colspan="2">Tools</th></tr>
<tr><td colspan="2">Programs, software, applications — call them what you will. As in life, we use Tools (hammers; saws and so on) to create things. On the Amiga we use tools to create music scores, artwork, documents and so on. This analogy tends to get stretched a bit because some tools do not actually create a finished product as such. MORE (on the Extras 1.3 disk) is a typical example — it is a Tool which allows you to view documents.</td></tr>
<tr><td>Snapshot</td><td>X and Y relative to window.</td></tr>
<tr><td>Info usage</td><td>Size; Status; Stack; Comment; Tool Types.</td></tr>
<tr><td>Example</td><td>Preferences</td></tr>
</table>

Projects	
These are the files created by Tools. Well-behaved Tools (such as DPaint) create a project icon for every drawing or brush you save. DPaint is a particularly good example because the picture and brush project icons look different.	
Snapshot	X and Y relative to window.
Info usage	Size; Status; Stack; Comment; Default Tool; Tool Types.
Example	Shell

Disks	
Disk icons are displayed automatically when you insert a disk the machine. Although the standard software supplied with the Amiga does not support it, these icons can get very large.	
Snapshot	X and Y relative to Workbench screen; size and position of first open window; view position (set by scroll bars).
Info usage	Size (disk info); Default Tool; Tool Types; Status (set by disk write protect).
Example	Workbench

Drawers	
Drawers represent directories in the AmigaDOS hierarchy. Using this analogy, the disk is the filing cabinet and drawers are part of it. However, drawers can contain drawers, which contain drawers, which also contain drawers and so on.	
Snapshot	X and Y relative to owners window; size and position of window; view position (set by scroll bars).
Info usage	Status; Comment; Tool Types.
Example	Utilities

<table>
<tr><th colspan="2">Garbage</th></tr>
<tr><td colspan="2">This is a special directory (drawer) used exclusively by the Workbench for the trashcan. For most purposes, the trashcan acts like any other drawer but Workbench knows when it has been selected and activates the Empty Trash menu item. When you operate Empty Trash, Workbench attempts to Discard everything in the drawer.</td></tr>
<tr><td>Snapshot</td><td>X and Y relative to owners window; size and position of window; view position (set by scroll bars).</td></tr>
<tr><td>Info usage</td><td>Status; Comment; Tool Types.</td></tr>
<tr><td>Example</td><td>Trashcan</td></tr>
</table>

Inside Info

Now you have a better understanding of how Workbench works — albeit at a very simple level — it is time to start looking at some of its hidden features.

Lesson 12
Using Get Info

You will need

☞ Your Workbench disk

1. Open the Workbench disk

2. Select the Utilities drawer

3. Now select Info from the Workbench menu.

After a short pause, a large window will open up and present you with a lot of information about the Utilities drawer. The bar at the top left of the screen is the name of the item you have selected information for — Utilities in this case. Just below that is the type of item: Drawer. If you have experimented with IconED on the Extras disk, you may have noticed there are several icon *types*: Tool, Project, Disk, Drawer and Garbage.

Each type has a different meaning to Workbench and can store its own snapshot information. It is important to know what these are if you are going to get the best from Workbench. A quick reference is listed at the end of this chapter. You can get information on any Workbench object simply by selecting it, then selecting Info from the Workbench menu. Each icon type has its own Info window, and although the contents vary, the same rules apply.

The Size Display

Projects, Tools and Disks have a size associated with them. Projects and Tools take up a certain amount of disk space; disks have a certain amount of space available. This area displays any relevant information. Drawers never display a size box — but this does not mean they are empty. In any case they still take up room on the Workbench disk.

The Status Flags

At the right-hand side of the display is a row of four gadgets used to control what are called the "protection" or status flags of the icon (and the object it refers to). Flags are binary bits — a bit like light switches — so they can be on or off. You can change the state of any of them just by clicking on them. Here is a list of the available flags and their meanings:

Archive: is provided for information only and is not used by Workbench. Setting (Archived) or resetting (Not Archived) this has no effect on the Workbench. Some software can force the flag on however.

Read: is not generally used in Workbench 1.3 — but some third-party software will act on it. This flag is best left in its default state: Readable.

Write: like read, is not generally used in Workbench 1.3.

Delete: is used by Workbench (at AmigaDOS level) and is the usual cause for heartache when trying to discard several icons or empty the trashcan. Setting this flag (Not Deleteable) helps to stop you discarding something by mistake. The snapshot function will not work while this flag is active — see below.

It is important to note here, icons are connected to objects (files) by name. While you remain in Workbench, the protection flags of both the object *and* the icon which belongs to it are affected by Info. Once you enter the Shell (AmigaDOS land folks) you get control over the protection flags of individual objects. This is where it gets confusing and is mentioned here because it can give rise to some peculiar errors with some third-party (usually PD) software.

The Comment Editor

Is reserved for you to add short comments about individual icons, and, although the maximum limit is 79 characters – 51 characters is the practical limit. It is a standard Amiga string gadget — these were discussed earlier for renaming disks and icons. Briefly to operate string gadgets you simply click in them and start typing. If the gadget already contains text, you can click anywhere in the text and insert more text. Pressing A-**X** clears the gadget.

The Default Tool Editor

Displays the default Tool for Project and Disk icons. For projects, this is the name and path of the Tool Workbench will *launch* when you double-click the icon. Disk icons use this to get the path and filename of the DiskCopy function called when you select the icon and select Duplicate. It always reads: SYS:System/Diskcopy. This gadget is reserved primarily for developers and advanced users. Most Tools will fix this for themselves; however this can give rise to odd errors when you double click the icon. You can change a Project's default tool if need be, but as a general rule of thumb, leave well alone.

The Tool Types Editor

The information stored in this gadget is passed to a Tool when it starts. The contents can vary greatly and are very application specific. Many Tools do not use this, but those that do often supply more than one option. IconX (new in release 1.3) is a typical example: it has two options WINDOW and DELAY. If you just want to view the current list, you can use the up and down arrows (left of the gadget). To add a new Tool Type, click ADD — right of the gadget; and to delete an old one, click DEL. Tool Types have no effect on Drawers.

Note: If your software's manual tells you to enter something in the Tool Types array say:
`WINDOW=CON:0/0/640/200/Turtlator.`

Do it exactly like that — unlike the rest of the Amiga system, Tool Types are sensitive to case — so entering Window= or wINDOW= would not work.

The Stack Editor

This is located just below the size display, in the Info for Projects and Tools is the number of bytes allocated to an application's process stack when it is launched by the Workbench. I have deliberately made that explanation complex as a warning: **DO NOT FIDDLE WITH IT!**

Basic Printer Preferences

The simplest and most common printers in use today are the 9-pin impact dot-matrix (IDM) variety. Although there has been an upsurge of ink jet and even laser printers recently (advances in print engine technology have seen to that) impact machines refuse to go away.

The actual mechanics of printing – even on a fairly simple level – are a marvel of modern technology, so this discussion will be simplified. As the name implies, dot-matrix printers draw characters from an array of dots. The number of dots in the matrix determines the quality of the final output; ergo, the more pins you have, the better the quality of print.

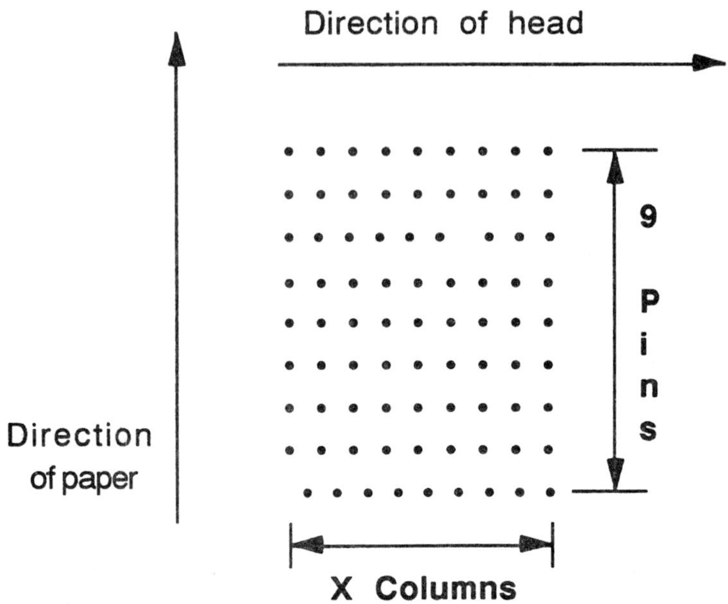

Take a typical 9-pin print head. Inside nine tiny, electrically operated – pins – are arranged vertically from top to bottom. Characters are printed by firing the pins as the head moves over the paper. As this happens, the pins hit the ribbon and punch it against the paper – depositing a small amount of ink on it. This all goes on at a mind-numbing speed and results in a screeching clatter as the pins fire hundreds of times per second.

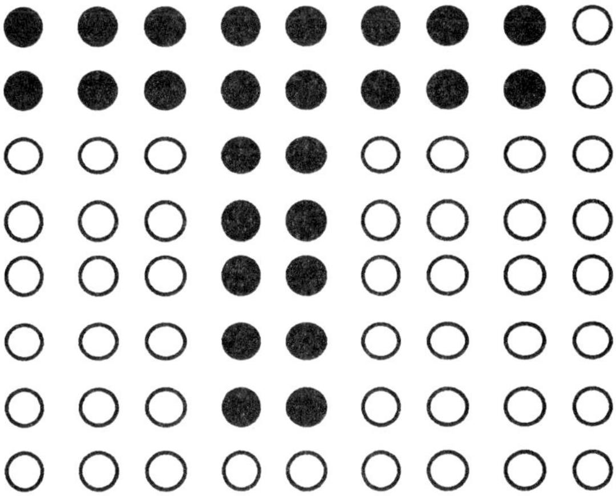

The letter T defined on a 9 pin matrix

Near Letter Quality (NLQ) printing is achieved in much the same way, but each character has two matrixes – one slightly offset from the other. Rows of characters are usually printed in two passes and only half of the matrix is printed each time. The print head moves much slower in NLQ mode so each dot can be printed twice.

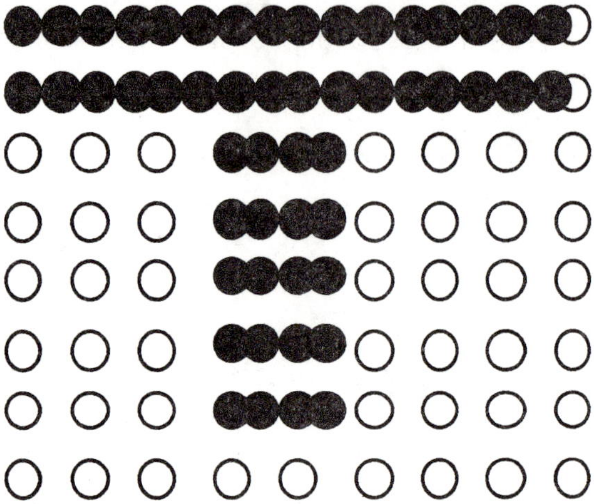

The letter "T" in NLQ

So What's a Printer Driver?

This question pops up all the time. Printer drivers address a specific problem which is this: there is no standard, universally accepted language for controlling printers. This might seem strange, especially since the Centronics printer port has been so widely accepted. But the Centronics interface only addresses the electronic connection between the computer and the printer. Software control of the printer is a completely different ball game.

At the text-only level, this is reasonably straightforward. You send ASCII (text) and the printer prints it. However, what about all the special effects? Double height, double width, superscript, subscript, and so on. Add colour to that lot and you enter a nightmare world of complexity.

Enter printer drivers. These act as interpreters — allowing software to communicate with printers in a language they both understand. Therefore, in order to get the best from your printer — this applies to graphics especially — you must use the correct driver. Some finer points may still require special coding sequences but this is largely software independent.

With all this complexity it's hardly surprising many beginners find the subject of printing something of a black (or should that be black and white) art. This chapter — and the next one — are a series of lessons concerned with getting *your* printer to work; or work better with the Amiga. They don't cover all printers — there's hundreds of them — but they should give you a better idea of what's going on. Later on you'll see how to access your printer under AmigaDOS control. But now, back to the basics:

Lesson 13
Installing A Printer Driver

You will need

☞ Your Workbench disk

☞ Your Extras disk

1. Open the Workbench disk
2. Open the Utilities drawer
3. Double-click on the InstallPrinter icon

4. Several disk swaps later you will be presented with a list of printer drivers. and a prompt which looks like this:

```
Which printer ? (Press RETURN to exit)
```

5. Select the correct driver (a list of printer drivers is given in the appendices).

6. Now either:

   a) enter the full name of the driver you want to use (say EpsonQ) and press Return (↵)*or* Enter.

```
Which printer ? (Press RETURN to exit) EpsonQ
```

   or:

   b) enter the first few letters of the name and add the characters #? to the end like this:

```
Which printer ? (Press RETURN to exit) EpsonX#?
```

Lesson 14
Setting Up A Printer

You will need

☞ Your Workbench disk

☞ Your printer's manual

Preferences received a significant enhancement for Workbench 1.3 (especially on the printers side) so this lesson will concentrate on that one. The 1.2 version is broadly similar only it's much slower and has fewer features.

Workbench's Preferences are a source of confusion — not least because the settings are unique to each Workbench (boot) disk. This could mean your Deluxe Paint boot disk is set up for Okimate 20 colour printer on the serial port — and your Scribble disk is set up for a 24 pin Epson printer on the parallel port. This would be an advantage because DPaint would use the colour printer, and Scribble, the high-quality dot-matrix. Few of us are lucky to own more than two printers, so here is a general guide for installing most common models.

1. Open the Workbench disk

2. Open the Prefs drawer

3a) If you have Workbench 1.3, you will be able to open Printer Preferences directly by opening the Printer icon. (Printer is a Project icon and shows the use of Tool Types and Default Tools discussed above.)

3b). If you are using an earlier version of Workbench (or the Printer icon is not present) open the Preferences tool, then click the Change Printer gadget in the bottom left of the screen.

4. If your printer is capable of printing graphics (most are) click on the Graphic Select or Graphic 1 gadget. Otherwise proceed to Step 8.

5. When the new screen appears you will have a choice of options which are too involved to explain at this stage. As a general rule. use colour - even if you have a black and white printer. Grey Scale 1 (or Grey Scale). Grey Scale 2 is only used for the A2024 monochrome monitor. Do not use the Black & White option unless you need to print in black and white. Threshold only effects graphics when the Black & White switch is on — so you can leave this alone.

6. The Aspect and Image settings are best left alone since they can give some unexpected results. As a guide, if your images are too wide to fit on the page, change the Aspect to vertical. The Image button can be set on Negative for monochrome printers if you are getting large amounts of black. Do not do this this with a colour printer, unless you are prepared for some unexpected results.

7. Once you are happy with the settings, click OK and return to the main screen. In case you think you might have altered something you didn't want to, just click Cancel and start again.

8. A list of printers should have appeared in the top left of the display — and your printer must be capable of emulating the one displayed and highlighted. The "custom" and "generic" options are special: generic is a plain text driver; custom is used by special drivers.

✓ Most common dot-matrix printers – especially budget ones – conform to Epson's standard. Unless you have an old Epson, try EpsonX[CBM_MPS-1250]. The more powerful, 24-pin machines can be driven by the EpsonQ driver (although the 9-pin EpsonX driver is better for graphics work). If your printer is not listed try using the InstallPrinter script supplied with your machine. Note: the Amiga can drive most common printers - see Appendix. If in doubt either read the printer's manual or try experimenting!

✓ If your work involves a lot of graphics printing, you should select a Paper Type of "Single Sheet". This helps avoid the worst of the banding (white lines) found on many dot-matrix printers. That includes the Oki-20 and the Star LC series. You can still use fanfold (computer) paper but single sheets give the best results.

Paper Size, length and other dimensions are a little too specific to give a guide for since every setup is different. As a rough guide, the Star LC10/200 series, CBM_MPS-1250, Epson FX/EX-80, Juki 5510/20, Panasonic KXP-1081, Citizen 120D and Okidata 292/293I come with narrow tractors. [OK, I know some are available with 15" tractors]. For general purpose computer paper you should set Length to 66 lines, Left margin at 1, and Right margin at 80. For wide tractor machines like the Star NB24-15 (assuming the paper is full 15" width) you could set a Right margin of 132.

Print quality is determined by the Quality buttons. You can change this, but most word processing software will override the settings.

Print pitch and **Line Spacing** are personal taste. For general word processing they are best left at 10-CPI (Characters Per Inch) and 6-LPI (Lines Per Inch). You can condense the number of characters to 12 or even 15 CPI if your printer supports it — most do — but you must adjust column width (left and right margins) and page length yourself. These settings have no effect on graphics printing and may be changed by your word processing software.

9. Finally click OK to return to the main Preferences screen and click the Save gadget to make your changes take effect.

A Spanner In The Preferences

When you have set and saved your Preferences they remain unique for that boot disk. If you booted DPaint or Scribble, the printer setup will be taken from that disk. To get around this Commodore supply a simple utility, CopyPrefs, which moves your settings to other disks. This suffers with two distinct problems.

- It only works on machines with two or more drives.
- It does not copy your default printer driver.

There is no easy way around this unless the software comes with a Workbench and its own Preferences tool — as a stopgap you should boot from your Workbench disk and start the offending application from there — be warned this is likely to cause a lot of disk swapping though. Lesson 27 (in Your First Boot Disk) contains more information on this subject.

Advanced Printer Preferences

Printers cause a lot of grief, so for those of you still having difficulty knowing which driver to use, Appendix XX, should make interesting reading. It lists all the popular printers (and some odd ones) known to work with the Amiga and the appropriate driver to use. Not all the drivers are complete emulations though. For instance, the MPS-1000 driver can be used with the incredibly cute Canon BJ-10e – but it cannot facilitate the 360x360 DPI graphics mode. This is because although the Canon emulates IBM graphics, it has extensions which the IBM driver does not know about. Don't worry if you are unsure what that means – all will be revealed shortly.

Lesson 15
Setting Printer Graphics

You will need

☞ Your Workbench disk

1. Boot your Workbench disk

2. Open the Preferences drawer

3. Double-click on the Printer icon

4. Click on the Graphic 2 box.

The screen is split into several sections but many of these affect each other – and this can be a source of confusion. Note: these options only affect graphics – but many DTP packages and Word Publishers – NotePad, Kind Words, Page Setter – to name just three can produce text using graphic dumps; so you should know how to operate them. Basically all the buttons work in much the same way as those you have already met in Preferences – so you can experiment by clicking on a few to watch the effects. Buttons are active when they are highlighted in orange (given the default palette). Some buttons – like RGB toggle; others – like density – act like radio buttons. That is, one must be selected all the time.

Density

Of all the options on Graphic 2, this is the most important for most applications. It determines the speed, darkness and resolution of the printing in dots-per-inch (DPI). Generally speaking, the larger the number the darker and slower the printing. However, only a few printers (or their drivers) support more than one or two densities.

This option carries a warning with it – although the manual is not clear on the point – **do not** select multi-pass printing if you are using a colour ribbon. Here's why. Colour ribbons come with three primary colours – red, blue, yellow; plus black. Now let's imagine you are printing some medium green – a field for example. First, the printer deposits a row of yellow dots, then a row of blue ones which mix to give a shade of green. The light colours are always printed first to avoid contamination.

On the second pass, the printer runs the yellow ribbon back over the existing green ink, and... the yellow ribbon becomes covered in fresh green ink. Because printer ribbons are only a few metres long (some are even shorter) just a couple of dumps could ruin a brand new – and expensive – colour ribbon.

Multi-pass printing is employed by the Epson FX (9-pin) series driver for densities greater than one. So if you have, for example, a Star LC-200C do not select a higher value unless you are only doing monochrome printing.

Just to confound matters, the density switch is tied to the single sheet/Fanfold option on the Graphic1 options screen. This only applies to 24-pin printers using the EpsonQ driver. When single sheet mode is selected, only 16 of the 24 pins are used. This option is provided (apparently) for printers with weak power supplies – characterised by fading horizontal stripes on dumps.

Dithering

This technique is widely used in newspapers to reproduce pictures from thousands of little dots – the greater the concentration of dots, the darker the image. The computer application is similar but the dither is produced mathematically and on the Amiga it comes in one of three exciting flavours; Ordered, Half-tone or Floyd-Steinberg.

Ordered dithering, the default method, is simple but not very effective and is best used on low-resolution printouts when the other methods are less effective. Just because you have a high-resolution printer though, does not mean it will be producing a high resolution dump. For instance the 9-pin Star LC-10 has a varying resolution from 60 to 240 DPI but in order to achieve the high resolution print, it has to perform multiple passes. Put another way, if you are printing in colour on these machines you **must** use ordered dither.

Halftone dithering is a method more like the one used by newspapers but it requires a higher resolution printout to get the best effect. Select a density over three for 9-pin machines and greater than one for 24-pins.

F-S or **Floyd-Steinberg** is the most effective dither – but incurs approximately a 50 per cent reduction in speed over the other methods. Like half-tone dithering, the Floyd-Steinberg method works best with high-resolution dumps; see half-tone above. Smoothing (see below) is not available with this technique – since it is inherent anyway. This form of dither is the most attractive to the eye and is usually characterised by the diagonal ripples or rivers which tend to appear in the printout.

Smoothing

This setting can be used to help even out the “jaggies” on diagonal lines and around circles. It does this by dithering around sharp edges. By nature of the technique, smoothing incurs approximately a 2:1 speed penalty and can only be used with ordered or half-tone dither. Smoothing works best on high-resolution printers but gives noticeable improvement to dumps produced at greater than 150 DPI. For 9-pin Epson machines set a density of four or five; for 24-pin models use a density of two, three or four.

Color Correct

This only applies to colour printing so if you have a monochrome only machine you can skip this bit. This option is a bit of a hoax if you happen to be working on a clapped out old colour telly because it attempts to match the colours on the printer more closely to those on the screen. The three buttons are individually selectable – each affecting shades of Red (R) Green (G) and Blue (B). There is a slight penalty in using these in that there is a reduction of 308 available (printed) shades for each correction highlighted.

The best way to see this option in action is to try it. Using your favourite art package, draw three rectangles; one each of red, green and blue. Now print it, set the colour on for all three guns and print the picture again. Compare the two dumps to see the difference.

Centre

When this option is selected the image will be printed horizontally centred on the page. This will only work if you have set the correct tractor width on the main printer preferences screen. Selecting this button overrides the Left Offset value (see below).

Left Offset

The distance from the left of the page where the printing will start. Measured in inches and tenths. This option defaults to 0.0" and is overridden by the centring switch. Note, this is a string gadget, so you should click once inside it – then enter the new value.

Scaling

Determines how the dump will be scaled to fit the page. The default is fractional which is suitable for normal artwork. When integer scaling is in effect, each dot on the picture will be represented as an exact number of dots on the page. This has some curious effects because it effectively overrides the aspect ration correction. However, it should be used when printing bit-image fonts such as those in NotePad and PageSetter to prevent them becoming garbed by fractional scaling.

Height and Width Limits

These determine the width and height of a printed picture in tenths of inches; pixels or a multiplication factor. When one of these is set to zero, the correct value will be calculated for you. In this way you can set the width of your picture and force the driver to maintain its correct height, and therefore, aspect ratio. Note: this is only accurate when fractional scaling is in effect.

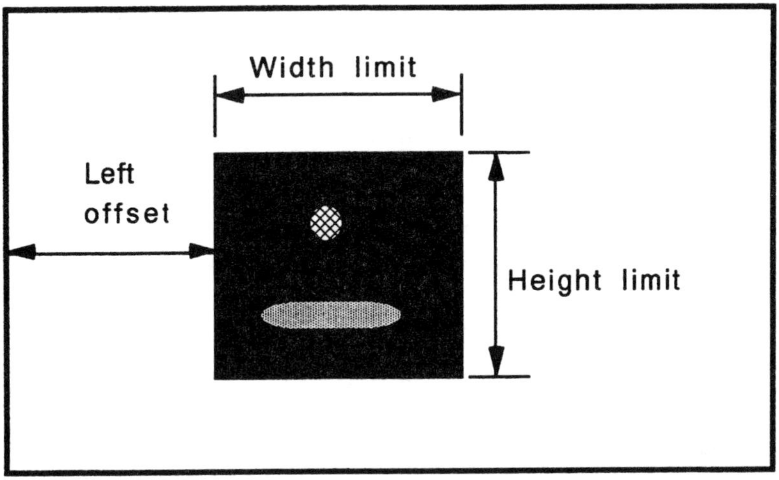

How the limits affect a picture

Limits

These switches determine how the width and height limits affect a picture.

Absolute: The picture's width and height is determined in inches by the limit settings. This is illustrated in above. For instance, to get a picture four inches wide, set a width of 40 and select absolute. If you leave the height set at zero the aspect ratio will be corrected automatically. This works in reverse too, but remember the paper for a narrow tractor printer is only about 8" wide.

Bounded: The image will be placed inside a bounding box of the width and height determined by the setting in the limits box. This differs from the absolute limits because the picture will be fitted inside the bounding box – not scaled to fit it. The size of the box is fixed in tenths of inches, so to get a bounding box 3" wide by 2" high, set width to 30 and height to 20.

Pixels: is exactly the same as the absolute option – but the width and height values are read as pixels instead.

Multiply: when this option is used, the values entered in the width and height boxes are used to multiply the number of pixels in the picture. For instance, if the picture is 320 X 256 and you entered 2 in the width box, the printed version would be 640 pixels wide – with the vertical aspect corrected accordingly.

Lesson 16
Get the Best From Graphics

You will need

☞ Your Workbench disk

☞ A suitable printer connected and ready to go

This lesson is more concerned with trial and error for getting the best effect. So, dust off your favourite art package and get drawing – because the best way to learn how the graphic options work is try them! NotePad can be used to good effect here. All you have to do is create a small document using a couple of different fonts and try printing them using the As Graphic option. The clever bit is you can alter the Preferences settings while NotePad is still active! This is how its done:

1. Open your Workbench disk.

2. Open the Prefs drawer.
3. Open the Utilities drawer.
4. Open the NotePad tool by double-clicking its icon.
5. Write a few lines of text – be bold, be wild, be beautiful – don't be afraid to experiment. If you have a colour printer, try selecting different inks.
6. Now select Print and see what happens.
7. Use the depth gadgets until you find the Prefs drawer and double click on the printer icon.
8. Select Graphic 2 and make some changes – read the notes above carefully if you are unsure what to do.
9. Click on OK to get back to the main window, click OK to get back to the Preferences screen then click on USE.
10. Now go back to NotePad – don't forget to click in its window to activate it and print your text again.
11. Make a note of the changes
12. Repeat steps 7..11 until you feel happy with what is happening.

Extras Fonts

Commodore supply three extra fonts on the Extras disk. Unlike the slightly quirky fonts supplied as standard, these are high-quality industry standard type faces from Adobe — the designers of Postscript. Times, for instance, was originally commissioned by the Times newspaper. Courier on the other hand is a simple — typewriter-like font — that has some unique uses. Courier is used for some of the examples in this book where the Shell's output is being printed. Here's some examples:

Times: The quick brown fox jumped over the lazy journalist

Helvetica: The quick brown fox jumped over the lazy journalist

`Courier: The quick brown fox jumped over the lazy journalist`

If you have not delved into the Shell before — then this is your chance. You're probably also wondering where the Fonts drawer is; well at Workbench level, it never appears — that is why this example is going to take you straight into the heart of AmigaDOS.

One of the cleverest things about AmigaDOS is it is possible to tell it *where* to look for its fonts. Fonts, not surprisingly perhaps, usually live on the boot disk's "Fonts" directory, but they could be anywhere — even on a completely different disk. This is the whole key, since fonts are a little disk hungry, you could have a disk containing nothing but fonts! That stuff is a little advanced yet, but the principal can be illustrated by this "simple" example.

Lesson 17
Getting More Fonts (part 1)

You will need

☞ Your Workbench disk

☞ Your Extras disk

1. Make a copy of your Extras 1.3 disk — the one with AmigaBASIC on. (Reminder: you can do this by clicking once on its icon and selecting Duplicate from the disk menu.)
2. Select the disk marked "Copy of Extras 1.3" and rename it **MoreFonts**. Letter case is not important, but it is vital you do not put a space between the words. (If the disk is not present on your Workbench, pop it in any drive.)
3. Replace Workbench in any drive and open the Shell icon.
4. The Shell window will appear with a "prompt" ready for you to enter commands. (If you have used an 8-bit machine such as the BBC or the C64 you will

already have used something similar.) The prompt will look something like this:

```
1.SYS:>
```

However, for the sake of clarity I'll adopt a simple prompt: "1> " to show you where to type something. Do not type the prompt, just what comes after it. At the end of the line press return to send the command.

5. Next you are going to write a simple AmigaDOS program — a script. Enter the following:

```
1>ED SYS:FontsPlus
```

after a short while a window will appear. This is ED — the AmigaDOS screen editor. FontsPlus is the name of the script program you are creating and SYS: before the name makes certain it goes in the main Workbench drawer — the root directory. If you have a word processor such as Protext you can use that.

6. Now type the following — exactly as it appears:

```
ASSIGN FONTS: MoreFonts:Fonts
```

Purists might argue letter case is not important — which is true — however, good use of upper and lower case letters make the meaning of a program clearer.

7. Press the key marked [ESC] this is normally referred to as Escape and is ED's main "command" key. When you do this an asterisk (*) will appear in the bottom left of the window.

8. Press the X key once. Notice how X appears next to the asterisk. Now press Return and the window will close. [ESC]-X or Escape-X is a way of telling ED you have finished and want to save the file just created. If you make a mistake and get confused, just press [ESC]-Q, then press Y to confirm you don't mind losing the changes (edits). Now just go back to step 5 and try again.

9. Well done! You have just created your first AmigaDOS script program. As it stands, this script is not very useful in that you have to run it from the Shell. Let's try that. If the MoreFonts (old extras disk) is still in an external drive, remove it now. You should be back at the Shell prompt so type this:

```
1>EXECUTE SYS:MoreFonts
```

A requester will appear asking you to "Replace volume MoreFonts in any drive" — don't — just press cancel. You should now get an error message:

```
ASSIGN failed returncode 20
```

If the requester does not appear, go back to 5 and check you have entered everything correctly.

10. Repeat step 9, but this time replace the MoreFonts disk (in any drive) when the requester appears. After a short time the requester will vanish and you will be returned to the Shell prompt. If the requester stays on screen select the cancel button, go back to step 5, and check you have entered everything correctly.

11. Assuming everything has gone according to plan, you will now have access to the Adobe fonts on the old extras disk. You can check this by entering the following command. (Single drive users will have to swap disks here; another good reason to treat yourself to that extra drive.) Shell's output is shown in **bold**:

```
1>DIR FONTS: FILES
Courier.font
Helvetica.font
Times.font
```

12. Now you need a second program, to put everything back the way it was! The technique is exactly the same — the only things that change are the command and the script name. For the sake of example, I'll call this script "OldFonts", therefore at the prompt enter:

```
1>ED SYS:OldFonts
```

And the program looks like this:

```
ASSIGN FONTS: SYS:Fonts
```

Otherwise, the remainder of the instructions are more or less the same. This script will tell AmigaDOS to use the standard set of fonts (from the current boot disk).

This is all fine and nice, but it does not really address the problem of making the extra fonts easily accessible from the Workbench. That is why this tutorial is split into several small sections, the next Lesson will use the scripts you have just created to do just that!

Lesson 18
More Fonts (part 2)
IconX and IconEd

You will need

☞ Your Workbench disk

☞ Your Extras disk

IconX (Icon eXecute) is a special program provided with Workbench 1.3 which allows you to run AmigaDOS programs — more accurately called scripts — from the Workbench. Experts use scripts to provide all sorts of extra features and even enhance AmigaDOS. This lesson is intended to demonstrate how to use IconX to provide you with a neat way to get extra fonts at the double-click of an icon.

If you have been following this lesson in sequence, you will have just created two small script files on your Workbench disk. To use these effectively from the Workbench without the hassle of dropping into a Shell, you must give them an Icon.

Icons are created in two steps. First the icon is designed and saved to disk, next it is attached to the program which requires it. Two tools are responsible for the creation of icons: IconEd and IconMerge. To keep things simple(r) at this stage, I'll only describe IconEd. The program lives in the tools drawer of your Extras disk — although you use the copy renamed MoreFonts earlier.

1. Open the preferences drawer on your Workbench disk
2. Drag the Printer icon into the RAM disk. (The reason for this will become apparent soon.)
3. Insert your Extras disk and open the Tools drawer.
4. Double click the IconEd icon to start it and press OK to get rid of the information requester.
5. Now select "Load data" from the "Disk" menu.
6. Click in the box under "Enter Icon Name" and press Left-Amiga and the X key. This deletes the entire line. Now enter:

```
RAM:Printer
```

and click the "Load Icon Image" gadget. This operation should load the image for Printer Preferences into the current frame. If the icon does not appear, go back to step 1 and try again.

7. Now you can select "Clear frame" from the "Misc." menu and start drawing! IconEd is best learned by experience — most of the features are self-explanatory — apart from load and save data!

8. When you are happy with the final result, select "Save data" from the "Disk" menu. Now give the icon the name:

```
RAM:FontsPlus
```

Now click on the "Frame and save" gadget. This is the best selection (unless you have define a very large icon). To frame your image: click at its top left corner, move the mouse so a frame surrounds the complete image, then click the mouse again.

9. Move the IconEd window out of the way so you can see the RAM Disk's icon. Open the RAM disk and have a look at your icon — try clicking it to see if the effect is right. Keep experimenting until you're happy — but remember you must close and re-open the RAM disk to see the new icon.

10. To finish, click on IconEd's close box (not forgetting to save the image first). Now copy your new icon to the Workbench disk by dragging it from the RAM disk onto the Workbench disk.

11. Open your Workbench disk and select the new icon. You may want to snapshot it into position first.

12. With the icon selected, choose Info from the Workbench's Workbench menu. Now click in the "Default tool" box — and replace:

```
SYS:Prefs/Preferences
```

with

```
C:IconX
```

13. Similarly, delete the contents of the Tool Types box — these are not required for this simple demonstration.

14. That completes the operation! Now double-click on your icon and a small IconX window will appear. After a short time, a requester will appear asking you to insert volume MoreFonts: (assuming of course, it's not already in one of the drives).

15. If all has gone according to plan, drag your new icon *back* to the RAM disk and start IconEd again.

16. Now select "Load data" but this time use the name: `RAM:FontsPlus`

17. Create a new icon (this time for OldFonts) and save it with that name.

18. Follow steps 7..10 but save the icon with the name OldFonts. When you're happy, just drag the icon back to the Workbench disk. There is no need to go through the remainder of the steps (unless you want to check the Info box) because the Default tool is saved along with the icon data.

19. When you reset the machine, and start using the fonts, you will have the normal set. To use the new fonts just open the FontsPlus icon — the program, will prompt you for the correct disks. Many applications (NotePad etc.) read the fonts when they first start, so you should open FontsPlus first. To put everything back to normal, just open OldFonts!

Getting Started With AmigaDOS

By now you will be a black-belt in the art of Workbench and starting to experiment more with your machine. This is good news but it also means you want to know more.

DOS is an acronym usually taken to mean Disk Operating System – but on the Amiga it means much more than that. AmigaDOS is a high-level, user interface to all the machine's devices – a *device* operating system. Devices can be real hardware entities, such as disks; *virtual devices* simulated in software like the keyboard and screen; or *logical device assignments* – hard disk partitions and disk names.

Although this may seem complex initially, it is beautifully simple in practice. The idea being, the user can talk to any device in the same way. In other words you can use the same command to copy text from disk to disk, as well as disk to screen or disk to printer.

This is an introduction to AmigaDOS. However, to keep things interesting, a good – if not comprehensive – knowledge of the Workbench is assumed. You should therefore understand basic terms like initialise, click, double-click, open and so on.

AmigaDOS vs. Workbench

Some of you will have upgraded to an Amiga after experience of other machines – many of which will have had some form of command line disk or tape operating system. For the sake of those only used to WIMP systems like Intuition, GEM or Windows, a few words of explanation. AmigaDOS commands are called from a command line interpreter.

This is a bit like older adventure games where the player described what they wanted to do using English commands: GET SWORD, READ LITTLE BOOK, THROW KNIFE AT WIZARD and so on. The latest adventures allow you to manipulate objects with a mouse in the same way as you would communicate with Workbench. Although the very thought of a system where you have to describe every action might seem a retrograde step, in practice it is exceptionally powerful.

Take an example from the Workbench. Imagine you have opened a text file with a viewer such as More. (Document icons are usually configured to do this for you.) You now decide to get a hard copy on the printer so you just drag the icon to the Printer.

But wait, the printer does not have a Workbench icon. (That is why the Workbench replacement, Jazzbench supplies device icons for the printer etc.) You can get round this by loading the file into a word processor – NotePad would do – and printing it from there. It is possible, but long winded. Once you get used to AmigaDOS, this sort of thing is a doddle!

Lesson 19
Getting at AmigaDOS

You will need

☞ Your Workbench disk

Without further ado it's time to investigate AmigaDOS proper. On Workbench 1.3, you can start the AmigaDOS command line interpreter by opening the Shell icon. (Workbench 1.2 User's will have to activate the CLI icon first from Preferences. The actual icon lives in the System drawer.)

After a few seconds a window will open — the Shell window. The Shell and CLI windows are actually AmigaDOS device emulations called *consoles*. Three different flavours are available with the various versions. The earliest still in use, supplied with Workbench 1.2, has no editing facilities whatsoever, save for the delete key. For Workbench 1.3 a new console device was added offering simple line editing and a history buffer – this one is used by Shell.

At the top left of the screen is the *prompt*. This is AmigaDOS's way of telling you it is ready and waiting for its next command. On CLI windows the prompt follows the following format:

```
x>
```

Where [**x**] is the current CLI process identity – the CLI number. The **>** is used as a separator but it can be changed.

Shell windows use a slightly different prompt:

```
x.nnnn>
```

Where [**x**] is the CLI number and [**nnnn**] is the current directory pathname. As before, the > symbol is just a separator. You may not understand what some of this means yet – but don't worry, AmigaDOS and the Shell are governed by the proverbial chicken and egg (EggShell?) learning curve.

Shell's initial prompt normally looks like this:

```
1.SYS:>
```

The prompt and the information it displays is rather arbitrary. Using one simple command (PROMPT) you could easily change it to:

```
Your wish is my command>
```

For the sake of clarity, I'll adopt a standard CLI prompt **1>** when introducing a command line. You must not type this.

Lesson 20
Giving Commands

You will need

☞ Your Workbench disk

You give commands to AmigaDOS in the form of written (typed) instructions but it will not act until you press either the Return (↵) or Enter key. Therefore, if you are instructed to enter the following command line:

```
1>DIR
```

You would press the following keys:

D

I

R

↵ or **Enter**

Also, many commands take optional parameters, called *arguments*. All arguments must be separated from the command and each other by at least a single space. Therefore, the following line:

```
1>DIR OPT A
```

Would be typed thus:

D

I

R

[Spacebar]

O

P

T

[Spacebar]

A

↲ or **Enter**

Lesson 21
First Commands

You will need

☞ Your Workbench disk

Probably the most important commands in AmigaDOS, at least at grass-roots level, are those concerned with directory and file – *object* – management. There are several of these but the most important two are **DIR** and **CD.** Even basic knowledge of these two commands will allow you to get started with AmigaDOS. Try this:

```
1>DIR
C (dir)
Devs (dir)
Fonts (dir)
L (dir)
Libs (dir)
S (dir)
AmigaBASIC  AmigaBASIC.info
```

AmigaDOS responds by listing the names of all the files and directories contained in the current directory. The example listing here is from a theoretical disk – your screen will look slightly different. The command gets its name from an abbreviation of DIRectory. Directories contained in this listing are highlighted with **(dir)** automatically.

➡ You can press the spacebar at any time to stop AmigaDOS producing written output. Printing can be restarted with the backspace (←) key. This can sometimes make commands appear to fail – watch out for this.

Lesson 21
Changing Directory

You will need

☞ Your Workbench disk

AmigaDOS operates what is known as a hierarchial filing system. This sounds rather grand, but like walking, it's very simple when you know how. Disks are organised into directories and every disk has at least one -called the *root* directory. The root directory is always at the top of the hierarchy. Directories appear on the Workbench disk as drawers – but prior to Workbench 2, it is not generally possible (or practical) to show all the directories as drawers.

A typical disk hierarchy is illustrated in below – it looks something like the roots of a tree. Notice how all the *sub-*

directories (siblings) connect back to the root directory by pathways or *paths*. This is rather like a family tree – and is in fact, where the analogies of hierarchies, parents and children come from. Sibling is just another term for child – the two are often used interchangeably.

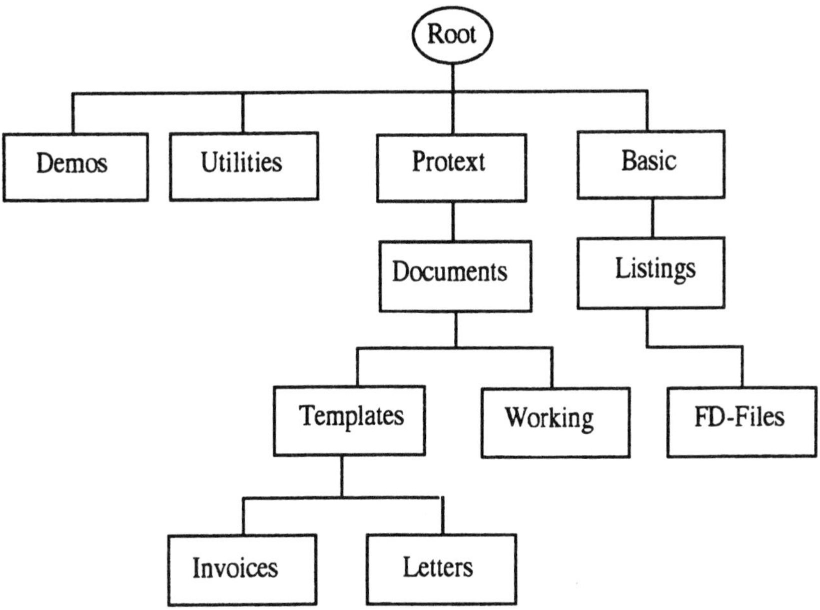

A typical disk hierarchy

AmigaDOS uses the / (slash) symbol to indicate a path and the : (colon) to indicate the root directory of any disk. Memorise these – you will use them a lot! Now study the slightly simplified version of the directory structure shown above. This time, the directory names have been replaced with letters and the *absolute paths* shown. Absolute paths can be used to get from any part of a disk hierarchy to any other. However, it is more usual to use the simpler method of *relative paths*.

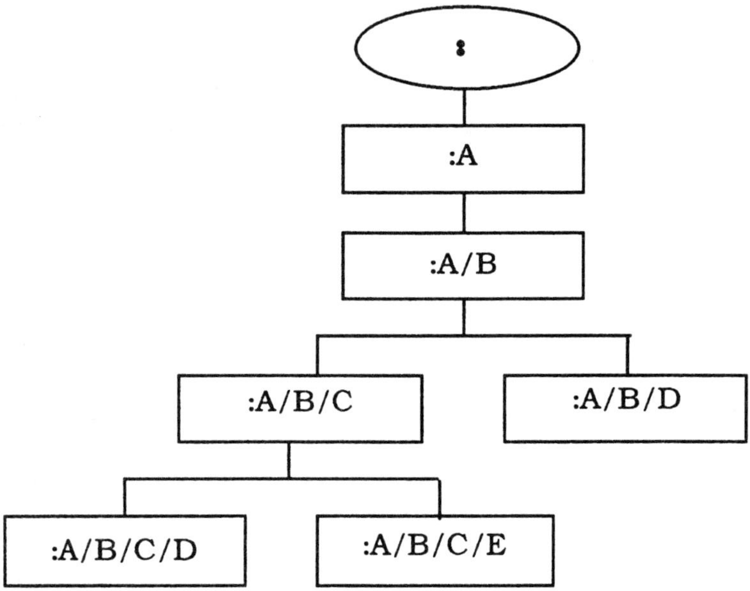

Simplified disk hierarchy showing paths. Root is shown by a colon. Note how directories in different part of the tree can have the same name.

At about this point many of you will be having a severe attack of *piuritus cerebrum*. – itchy brain. Relax – that is all just background knowledge which will become clear in time.

Before learning how to change directory, it is better to know how to find out *where* you are. This is achieved with the CD (Change Directory) command like this:

```
1>CD
Workbench1.3:
```

Workbench1.3 shown here is current *volume* (disk) name and the position in the hierarchy (:) or root directory. CD and AmigaDOS being the weird beasts they are, could have easily replied:

```
1>CD
SYS:
```

Which in this case mean precisely the same thing because Workbench1.3 was also used as the boot disk. The name *SYS* is a *logical device name* which was *assigned* automatically to the boot disk on startup. Once again, some of these terms may be a little unclear at the moment, but it is vital you understand the concepts giving rise to these – even if they fail to mean anything at this stage.

In order to move into a directory you must know the name of the directory you want to go to. This can normally be found by performing a DIR on the disk first. Try this:

```
1>CD DEVS
```

Which in English reads: "Change current directory to DEVS." The name **DEVS** is passed to the CD command as an argument. AmigaDOS1.3 users will notice the prompt also changes to indicate this. Just to confirm where you are type CD again:

```
1>CD
Workbench1.3:Devs
```

Notice how the case of the letters might differ from what you type. AmigaDOS is not sensitive to case, but object names are. The directory name is shown as it appears on the disk.

Lesson 22
Single Drives and Volumes

AmigaDOS uses a system of transient commands. This means every time you execute an AmigaDOS command it is loaded from disk, executed, then flushed from memory.

This might seem a little ludicrous because it gives rise to a lot of disk swapping; especially if you only have a basic machine with one drive. Transient commands are used because they save an enormous amount of memory and are easy to update. Imagine if DOS was on ROM and DIR had a serious bug – this would create havoc because ROMs have to be physically replaced by qualified engineers. As it is, bugs can be fixed by simply releasing a new version on a floppy disk.

So much for the advantages but this gets a little tiresome when using AmigaDOS on a single drive machine. Take the following example:

```
1>DIR DF0:
```

First, let's break this line down into its component parts:

DIR an AmigaDOS command to list the directory contents.

DF0: the device name for the internal drive – Disk Floppy 0. Note how device (and volume) names are *always* post-fixed with a colon. This acts as a separator and indicates the root directory of all filing system (data storage) devices.

Used in this way, AmigaDOS tries to read the root directory of the disk in the internal drive. This is fine if the disk just happens to be your startup disk, but try executing this command with a different disk.

Unless you are lucky enough to be using a hard disk, AmigaDOS responds with a requester asking you to replace volume xxxx (usually Workbench – the boot disk) in any drive. Single drive users are then confronted with a paradox: on replacing the boot disk in DF0: the machine reads the directory from that disk!

This happens because AmigaDOS knows its transient commands – DIR in this case – are located on the boot disk and asks for it back. When the disk is replaced, DIR is loaded and executed. However, the command line argument is interpreted by DIR – and because it says DF0: the disk loaded in DF0: at that precise moment is read.

There are several ways round this problem. Which you use depends on the version on AmigaDOS installed on your machine, the amount of memory and how well you label your disks! The simplest method works with all versions of AmigaDOS and works even when memory is tight. The command looks something like this:

```
1>DIR DF0: ?
NAME,OPT/K,ALL/S,DIRS/S,INTER/S,FILES/S:
```

What makes this command special is the use of a trick. Most AmigaDOS commands have an *interactive* mode – triggered by the query (?) operator. (Interactive mode can be used for some very advanced techniques which force AmigaDOS to do things automatically.) For the sake of this example, interactive mode has two important features. First, it offers a reminder of the command's options; second it forces it to load and wait – this is what makes it so useful.

Consider the previous example where AmigaDOS always lists the directory of the boot disk. If ? is specified before pressing Enter, AmigaDOS asks for the boot disk but the command halts and waits for user input. At this point you can swap to the disk you want a directory of and press Return.

This is not unlike using a sledge-hammer to crack a nut – but it works and conserves memory at the same time. A better technique, certainly a better behaved approach, is to use a volume name. A volume name is the name you give the disk after formatting it – not necessarily the name on the label! For instance to get a directory of the Extras disk you could enter:

```
1>DIR Extras1.3:
```

As before, the command is loaded from the boot disk – but instead of listing the contents of the disk in DF0:, AmigaDOS asks you to "insert volume Extras1.3 in any drive". The problem with this approach is brought about by Workbench and AmigaDOS allowing spaces in object names – disk names in this case. Let's say you had a disk called: Copy Of Workbench1.3, the following line will not work:

```
1>DIR Copy Of Workbench1.3:
```

because AmigaDOS thinks the disk is called "Copy" and the rest of the line are arguments. Remember how arguments are separated from the command and each other by spaces. The solution is to surround the volume name in quotes:

```
1>DIR "Copy Of Workbench1.3:"
```

At this stage, you may wonder why bother to use volume names at all? If you have more than one drive they seem pointless and long winded. What you use is up to you, but both methods have pros and cons. Device names are shorter *but* disk names are more reliable. This is particularly true when it comes to programming AmigaDOS and you want to make sure you are working on the correct disk

Lesson 23
Resident Commands

You will need

☞ Your Workbench disk

The variations just described rely on pre-loading the command before executing it. This is fine for commands you only need once in a while, but what about those in constant use. What is needed is a method which avoids all the constant disk swapping. Prior to AmigaDOS 1.3 there was only one method – and while it is a little clumsy, it is useful to know. The solution adopted in AmigaDOS 1.3 is better so I'll look at that one first.

All the AmigaDOS commands are stored in a special directory on the boot disk called C. At boot time this directory is given (assigned) a logical volume name of C:. Because of this, the AmigaDOS command directory can be accessed as if it were a normal disk volume, for instance:

```
1>DIR C:
1>CD C:
```

Given this knowledge you can make use of a special command introduced for AmigaDOS 1.3. As its name implies, RESIDENT, is used to pre-load copies of AmigaDOS commands into RAM. Once loaded in this way, commands stay in memory until you re-boot the machine. A typical synopsis for this command – making DIR resident is:

```
1>RESIDENT C:DIR
```

Note how you must specify the AmigaDOS command directory (C:) as part of the command line. This is so RESIDENT knows where to load the command from. To find out which commands are already resident:

```
1>RESIDENT
Name          UseCount
DIR           0
CD            0
RESIDENT      1
EXECUTE       0
```

Notice how each command has a UseCount figure. This is defined by the number of processes sharing each command. At this stage only, RESIDENT is showing a value of one, because the current (multi-tasked) process is using it; the other commands are idle. Multi-tasking is beyond the scope of this volume though. For now, why not try experimenting with some of the commands in the C: directory and making a few resident.

Workbench item	AmigaDOS Equivalent
Disk icon	Volume or disk + disk.info
Drawer icon	Directory (plus dot-info file)
Menu	None
Project icon	Data file (plus dot-info file)
Trashcan	Trashcan directory (plus dot-info file)
Tool icon	Program file (plus dot-info file)
Workbench window	Shell/CLI window

The Workbench items and AmigaDOS terms

Operation	AmigaDOS Equivalent
Clean up	None (only affects icons)
Close	CD
Discard	DELETE
Duplicate	COPY (files) or DISKCOPY (disks)
Empty Trash	DELETE
Info	STACK, LIST and INFO
Initialise	FORMAT
Last Error	WHY
Move (drag)	COPY or RENAME
Open	CD
Put in trash	RENAME
Redraw	None (only affects icons)
Remove from trash	RENAME
Rename	RENAME (files) or RELABEL (disks)
Snapshot	None (only affects icons)
Version	VERSION

Workbench operations and their closest AmigaDOS equivalents.

Practical AmigaDOS

The temporary method for getting access to the Adobe fonts (covered in the IconX tutorial) is fine, but the permanent solution is less hassle if you can make enough room on your Workbench disk.

Before you start, take a look in the Utilities drawer on your Workbench disk and see if there is anything you don't use very often. CMD, ClockPtr and Clock are typical candidates for the Trashcan.

Lesson 24
More Fonts (part 3)

You will need

☞ Your Workbench disk

☞ Your Extras disk

1. Open the Shell prompt.

2. Put your Workbench disk in df0:

3. At the prompt (1>) type the following (the Shell's output is shown in bold for clarity):

```
1>INFO df0:
Unit Size Used Free Full Errs Status Name
df0: 880K 1560 200 89% 0 Read/Write Workbench
```

The number you should be looking at is the the number of blocks free — you will need at least 198. This disk has 200 blocks available which is just (barely) enough. Fonts, like any files take up room on the disk, and the Adobe fonts have a more professional feel to them. Therefore, since you are in the Shell — you can remove of any fonts you don't like or never use! If you already have enough free space you can skip to 7.

4. For example, let's assume you wanted to get rid of the entire Sapphire font — you would enter:

```
1>DELETE FONTS:sapphire all
```

5. It is also possible (but more difficult) to remove just certain sizes. Every font has two entries in the FONTS: directory. A dot-font file and a font sub-directory which contains the actual definitions. You can see how this works by entering the following:

```
1>DIR FONTS: ALL
Courier (dir)
 11                    13
 15                    18
 24
[etc.]
```

6. The larger numbers are the files belonging to the bigger type faces. Large fonts take up more room on the disk, so you might just want to delete some of the larger ones: For instance, lets say you wanted to remove the large Diamond font — diamond 20:

```
1>DELETE FONTS:diamond/20
```

7. Adding the Adobe Fonts

When you have cleared enough room on your Workbench disk, the following command will duplicate all the fonts provided on your Extras disk onto your Workbench. Note, this command line is quite complex so you should be careful to get all the spaces in the right places. The quotes around the *source* directory (Extras 1.3:/fonts) are required because the volume name "Extras 1.3" has a space in the middle.

```
1>COPY "extras 1.3:fonts" to fonts: all
Courier.font..copied
Helvetica.font..copied
Times.font..copied
 Courier (dir) [created]
 11..copied
 13..copied
 15..copied
```

[and so it goes on until you are finally returned to the CLI prompt.]

Now type:

```
1>FIXFONTS
1>ENDCLI
```

You will now be returned to the Workbench and the new fonts will be ready for use. Purists will probably argue FIXFONTS is not required unless you have changed contents of one of the fonts directories. However, it only takes a few seconds to run and makes sure any changes you may have made are taken into account. The ENDCLI command just shuts down (closes) the Shell window. You can leave it open if you want to experiment a bit more.

Lesson 25
Adding a new AmigaDOS command

You will need

☞ Your Workbench disk

By now most of you should have managed to get standard applications like Workbench and DPaint printing to your satisfaction — but some non-standard (usually public domain) disks are likely to cause difficulties. Printers cause all sorts of problems, so this chapter includes some more guidelines for printer owners.

Those of you who haven't got a printer yet need not worry, there is something here for everyone including some more guidance in use of the AmigaDOS [1] interface. This is not a full tutorial on AmigaDOS, but these instructions are necessary to overcome some of the more irksome printer problems.

These problems are understandable, and not always easy to get round — and the best cures require knowledge of the Shell/CLI. These instructions will, therefore, be general hints to get you going.

Printers are controlled by some very clever software — which is what makes them appear so complex. Once you have configured a Workbench disk, printing directly from that is usually quite simple. Problems start to crop up when you want to print a file from another disk; especially if you have to boot from it first. So far, I have only addressed the major sticking point with Workbench 1.3, the printer driver — but there is more to it than that.

---

[1] There is a very close relationship between AmigaDOS and Workbench — in fact, the Workbench is, more or less, just a graphical interface to AmigaDOS! However, many operations normally performed from the Workbench can be enhanced or simplified from AmigaDOS. In fact, some operations are simpler from the Workbench- although many purists will probably write to their MP at the very idea!

Consult Tables 1 and 2. These are a greatly simplified comparison (looking from Workbench's side of the fence) of how the two relate. At first glance this might be enough to make you hang up your keyboard and stay with a mouse; or even give up computers and retire to a Tibetan monastery. To use a cliche, don't panic. It really is quite straightforward once you get the hang of entering simple commands.

For now, we'll use a bit of Shell trickery to help you get started printing files from other disks; this lesson will give you a chance to see how programs like MakeAuto are designed. It also has a side effect of making two often used commands more easily available. Two methods are outlined here, use whichever you feel most comfortable with. If you are still tied down with Workbench 1.2, this will not apply to you — because you do not have a Shell. Don't despair, skip to the third method which can be used from any version.

Method One — using ED

1. Open the Shell icon.

2. At the prompt type the following

```
1>ED S:Shell-startup
```

3. You have just told AmigaDOS to edit a command file — a script — which controls the behaviour of your Shell. This is a complex looking file, so for now just press the down cursor key until the block gets to the end of the file. Now enter the following three lines:

```
RESIDENT C:DIR
RESIDENT C:COPY
ALIAS PRINT COPY [] TO PRT:
```

4. Now press the key marked ESC. Note how the cursor block jumps to the * at the bottom of the screen. Press X *then* Return and ED will save the modifications and exit. You may have to write enable your Workbench disk to do this.

5. That completes the change — you only have to do this once. Now close the Shell by entering:

```
1>ENDCLI
```

Method Two — Using Redirection

1: This method is the fastest but it is error to prone (*arhum!*).

2: At the Shell prompt (**1.SYS>**) type the following exactly. This method writes directly to the file — if you make a mistake, however slight, use (ED) described above, to fix it.

```
1>ECHO >>S:Shell-startup "RESIDENT C:DIR"
1>ECHO >>S:Shell-startup "RESIDENT C:COPY"
1>ECHO >>S:Shell-startup "ALIAS PRINT COPY [] TO PRT:"
```

3: Finally close the Shell using the ENDCLI command.

Method Three — ED on Workbench 1.2

This method will work on all versions of Workbench, but, is not recommended for later versions. These instructions are stripped down, if you need more help with ED refer to Method One above.

1. Open the CLI icon.

2. At the prompt type the following

```
1>ED S:CLI-startup
```

3. Insert the following lines at the end of the existing file:

```
MAKEDIR RAM:C
COPY C:CD RAM:C
COPY C:DIR RAM:C
COPY C:COPY RAM:C
PATH RAM:C ADD
```

4. Now press ESC, X and Return to make ED save the modifications and exit. You may have to write-enable your Workbench disk to do this. Now close the CLI with the command:

```
ENDCLI
```

Lesson 26
Using PRINT from Workbench disks

You will need

☞ Your Workbench disk

☞ A printer

Whichever method you used, your Shell has just received a new command — a new AmigaDOS command in effect — PRINT, which will allow you to print any *plain* text file.

Plain means text without extra printing codes — these will be the majority.

The text viewer PPMore is sometimes used to view *packed* text files — PRINT will not work with those, unless you unpack them first with Power Packer. (Power Packer is a widely available Shareware — Version 3 is commercial — utility that you should get if you use a lot of PD software.) As a rule, if the file uses MORE (look at the icon's DEFAULT TOOL) you can use PRINT on it.

1. Open the Shell (CLI for 1.2 Workbench). This will take slightly longer than usual because new commands are being added.

2. Now pop the disk you want to print from into the internal drive. Open it from the Workbench and look for the icon you want to print. It could be called "READ ME 1st", "Readme.doc" or something similar. For this example, let's assume you want to print the file called, READ ME and it is stored in the DOCS drawer.

3. Now enter this [2]:

```
1>CD DF0:
```

That makes sure AmigaDOS knows you have changed disk.

---

[2] Many of the descriptions in this text refer to the internal drive or DF0:. This is fine for most machines which only have a single internal drive. If you have an A1500 you'll have two internal drives, DF0: is the one you boot Workbench from.

4. Now you need to check which drawer you want. (If the file you want to print is in the disks first window, you can skip this.) Enter the following — AmigaDOS's response is shown in **bold**— but remember, every disk is different:

```
1>DIR OPT D
C (dir)
DOCS (dir)
SOURCE (dir)
S (dir)
```

5. You can see there are four entries here, but only two had icons on the Workbench display: DOCS and SOURCE — and where are all those other icons? This is quite normal. Used in this way the DIR command only lists directories (drawers on Workbench) and items only appear if they have an icon associated with them. The directory you are interested in is DOCS, so the following command will enter that directory.

```
CD DOCS
```

6. Now we'll use DIR again to discover what is in this directory. From the Workbench, this fictional disk only displays one file — READ ME. But what else is in there?

```
1>DIR
Programmer Notes
READ ME
```

```
READ ME 2
READ ME.info
.info
```

7. It is quite common for extra files to get stuck willy-nilly on PD disks like this and they are often worth investigation. The file you are interested in is READ ME. As a matter of interest, any files marked nnnn.info are icons — the pictures displayed by Workbench; the blank .info is a private Workbench file.

8. Finally, you can print the file. If you are using Workbench 1.3 and have made the modification outlined above, you could enter the following:

```
1>PRINT "read me"
```

the alternative method, which you must use if you are using Workbench 1.2 is:

```
COPY "read me" PRT:
```

9. The preceding steps will soon become second nature, in fact, once you become well-versed with AmigaDOS you will see there are many short cuts. For instance, you could have popped the disk in drive 0 and entered for Workbench 1.3:

```
1>PRINT "df0:docs/read me"
```

or, for all versions:

```
1>COPY "df0:docs/read me" PRT:
```

but that assumes a certain amount of prior knowledge — such as where the file is located.

Lesson 27
Printer Vice

You will need

☞ Your Workbench disk

☞ Your Extras disk

Your printer is known to the Amiga as a *device*. In order to use it therefore, you need the software to control it — called a device driver. The printer's device driver in turn uses some other files which tell it: what type of printer it is; where to find it; and how to control it.

With the exception of the control file (the printer driver) all these are already present on the Workbench. This is not the case with all disks — and is why you have to use AmigaDOS to print some text files.

Many of you are still naturally fearful of AmigaDOS and prefer to use utilities such as SID, might want to print from PPMore. Both these are quite capable of printing *provided* that the boot disk is correctly set up. This problem occurs frequently, sometimes because there is insufficient room on the disk for the required files, or more often in the case of PD compilations, because someone was too lazy to check.

The following files are directly involved in controlling your printer:

printer.device

parallel.device [3]

system-configuration

[a specific printer driver]

To add complexity to confusion, all of these must be in the correct directories and the printer driver named in system-configuration must be present too! It is possible to write a program to check if a boot disk is capable of supporting a printer, but it is much simpler to use AmigaDOS; it is not possible from the Workbench.

However, before even attempting to make the disk suitable for use with a printer, you must first ensure there is enough room. In the worst case, if all the files and directories are missing, you need at least 92 blocks free. You can discover this by inserting the disk, clicking its icon, and selecting INFO from the Workbench menu. Even if there are less than 92 blocks, you may still be able to use the disk, but things start getting a little tight.

Assuming there is enough space available, proceed as follows:

1.

---

[3] Serial.device is used for serial printers

a) Workbench 1.3 owners should open the Shell and enter:

```
1>RESIDENT C:MAKEDIR
```

b) Workbench 1.2 users should use this instead. This assumes you have made the modification to CLI-Startup outlined above. If not, do that first.

```
1>COPY C:MAKEDIR RAM:C
```

2. Next, you need to make two new directories. These may already be present on the target disk, but this just creates a harmless error message "nnnn already exists" where nnnn is the name of the directory. Put the target disk in drive 0 and enter:

```
1>MAKEDIR DF0:DEVS
1>MAKEDIR DF0:DEVS/PRINTERS
```

3. Now you'll need to check which printer driver you have installed. You could just use Preferences, but there is a faster way. Put your Workbench disk in any drive and type the following (AmigaDOS's output is shown in bold):

```
1>TYPE >RAM:SC DEVS:System-configuration OPT H
1>SEARCH RAM:SC 80:
9 0080: 4570736F 6E585B4E 424D5F4D 50532D31
EpsonX[CBM_MPS-1
```

4. On the left of the display is the name of the printer driver set in preferences — long names are truncated when shown like this, but it's OK. Make a note of the name, you'll need it shortly. Now we'll set the directory to the printers sub-directory on the target disk, so place it in the *internal* drive and enter:

```
1>CD DF0:devs/printers
```

5. Now, remember at step 3, you saw the name of the printer driver in your preferences settings? You can use that information to copy the right printer driver to the target disk. Here's how. Just enter the line below, replacing "EpsonX[CBM_MPS-1" with the name you saw:

```
COPY devs:printers/EpsonX[CBM_MPS-1#? ""
devs:printers/EpsonX[CBM_MPS-1250]..copied
```

6. The next job is to replace the system-configuration (user preferences) file — the preferences settings on the target disk with your preferences. (Multi-drive users can use CopyPrefs to do this.) To do this enter the following:

```
CD DF0:devs
COPY DEVS:System-configuration ""
```

➠ It is possible (but unlikely) you will get an error at this point saying the file is protected from deletion.

If this happens, enter the following command and try again.

```
PROTECT System-configuration RWD
```

7. Next you need to copy the printer device driver software. This comprises of three files but only two are needed for most setups.

a) First, the printer software, which is always required.

```
COPY DEVS:Printer#? ""
```

devs:printer.device..copied

b) The printer device selectively calls one of two other "device drivers" — one parallel printers, the other for serial printers. Most of you will be using parallel printers so you can use this:

```
COPY DEVS:Parallel#? ""
```

devs:parallel.device..copied

If you have enough room, or are using a serial printer use this:

```
COPY DEVS:Serial#? ""
```

devs:Serial.device..copied

This information does not create a boot disk, but it will convert a bootable disk into one you can print from — assuming the applications already on the disk allow it. Even so, there is more than one way to skin a printer, for instance it is possible to create a "print file" which can be printed at a later time — even on a different day, or a completely different machine!

Your First Boot Disk

One of the most commonly asked questions is, "How do I create a boot disk?" and although this is one of the most potentially difficult and disastrous areas, here is a blow-by-blow example creating a boot disk tailored for the NotePad. There isn't room here to explain exaclty what everything does, but you'll soon get the hang of it. You must complete each step before proceeding to the next.

➠ In all the lessons, where you are required to enter something directly into the Shell, the Shell's initial prompt (1.SYS>) will be shown too in a simplified form. For instance, if you see:

```
1>DISKDOCTOR DF0:
```

you would enter (remember the 0 is a zero not an O):

```
DISKDOCTOR DF0:
```

Shell's output and responses are shown in bold face, viz:

```
1>DISKDOCTOR DF0:
Disk Doctor 1.3.4
Insert disk to be corrected and press RETURN
```

Finally, the symbol:

[etc.]

is used to indicate where AmigaDOS will produce a long list of information. When you have that firmly embedded in the ol' grey matter, you are ready to start mucking with AmigaDOS.

Lesson 28
Duplicate the Workbench 1.3 disk.

You will need

☞ Your Workbench disk

☞ A blank disk

The following instructions assume you have booted with a copy of Workbench and have opened the Shell window.

There are two ways to create a boot disk. Either create one from scratch or start with an existing one and change it to suit you; and this is the approach I'll adopt here.

1. Click in the Shell's window to make it active.

2. Users with two or more drives proceed to step 1.5

3. Enter the following at the prompt:

```
1>DISKCOPY FROM DF0: TO DF0
Place SOURCE disk ( FROM disk ) in drive DF0:
Press RETURN to continue
```

The FROM disk mentioned here is the Workbench disk already in the internal drive. After a short while AmigaDOS will prompt:

```
Place DESTINATION ( TO ) disk in drive DF1:
Press RETURN to continue
```

4. At this point you should replace your Workbench disk with the blank disk you dug out earlier and then press the Return (↵) or Enter key. It is *not* necessary to format (initialise) the disk first, AmigaDOS will do that for you. When the operation has been completed (this may take several disk swaps depending on how much RAM you have) Now continue to the next lesson.

5: Users with dual or multiple drives. (On the A1500, B2000 and A3000 machines the first external drive is called DF2, not DF1 as described here. The example remains the same, just substitute DF1 with DF2.)

```
1>DISKCOPY FROM DF0: TO DF1:
Place SOURCE disk ( FROM disk ) in drive DF0:
Place DESTINATION ( TO ) disk in drive DF1:
Press RETURN to continue
```

6. Leave the Workbench disk in the internal drive and place the blank disk in the external drive. It is *not* necessary to format (initialise) the disk first, AmigaDOS will do that for you.

Lesson 29
Rename the Disk

You will need

☞ Your Workbench disk

☞ The disk created in the previous lesson

Every time you duplicate a disk using the Workbench, the phrase "Copy of" gets appended to its name. Under AmigaDOS however, every copied disk retains its original name. AmigaDOS can tell the difference by using the disks internal "last modified" time and date stamp. Humans of course, fallible as we are, cannot. Therefore although it is quite possible to work on two disks of the same name, it is better to rename one of them; and that is the purpose of this step.

1. Single drive users especially should ensure a write-protected, working copy of Workbench is in the internal drive. You can check this by entering:

```
1>LIST SYS:
Directory "SYS:" on Tuesday 27-Aug-91
Expansion.info    894 ----rwed
.info              70 ----rwed
```

[etc.]

The command itself and the output are not really important. However, this command will make certain you are working with the right disk — the word **SYS:** tells AmigaDOS to check the current Workbench or boot disk. If any other disk is present in a single drive setup, AmigaDOS will display a request for the correct disk.

2. At this point you can even ask AmigaDOS to check if the disk in the internal drive is write protected, like this:

```
1>INFO DF0:
Unit  Size  Used Free   Full  Errs  Status       Name
DF0:  880K  1272   486   72% 0      Read Only Work
```

Once again, much of the information presented here is of no relevance yet. Two things can be seen from this example: under the status line the disk shows Read Only — write protected in other words. Also, its name is shown — Work in this case, a copy of Workbench. Simple names come in handy as you will see later. Users with multiple drives should proceed to the next lesson.

3. Now those (optional) steps are over it's time to rename the disk. Since you only have a single drive, I'll use a little trick.

```
1>RELABEL DRIVE DF0: NAME BOOT ?
DRIVE/A,NAME/A:
```

When the prompt "DRIVE/A,NAME/A" appears, replace the new disk — the copy of Workbench — in the internal drive *before* pressing Return. That's one way, here's another:

```
1>RELABEL ?
DRIVE/A,NAME/A: DF0: BOOT
```

In this case you enter the drive number and the disks name at the prompt; again changing the disk just before pressing Return for the second time. Continue to the next Lesson.

4. Renaming any disk with two or more drives is a simple matter of specifying the drive containing the disk and its new name. Making sure the Workbench disk is in the internal drive and the copy of it is in the external one enter this:

```
1>RELABEL DRIVE DF1: NAME BOOT
```

Assuming everything goes to plan, AmigaDOS will just return you to the prompt. You can check the disk's name has changed using the INFO command described above. Note, it will not appear on the Workbench screen until you:

a) Remove and re-insert the disk or,

b) Use the DISKCHANGE command to let Workbench know immediately. This command is rarely used, so I'll not detail it here.

Lesson 30
Remove unwanted directories

You will need

☞ Your Workbench disk

☞ The disk created in the previous lesson

At this stage, you have a complete and fully working Workbench disk called "boot". This may seem a trifle pointless but it avoids a lot of fiddling around with the things you normally take for granted. For instance, you set things like screen colours, printer settings and serial options through the preferences screen. But none of the options will work unless certain directories are present.

Virtually everything the Amiga does is controlled, at least in part, by software stored externally on the Workbench disk. Some of those items are required, others are not. Generally speaking drawers visible from the Workbench (Utilities, Empty etc.) are not usually required by the system so they can be discarded. Everything I am about to describe in this section can be easily performed from Workbench with judicious use of the Discard and Trashcan facilities; however, you should use AmigaDOS to get an idea of the contrast.

1. No matter how many drives you have, boot the machine with the disk just created — this serves to make the example easier to follow.

2. Next, you need to know which files and directories can be safely removed and which cannot. In most systems, the following drawers — known in AmigaDOS as directories — can be thrown away: Trashcan; Prefs; Empty; Expansion; Utilities. In

addition to those certain files in the System drawer can be removed.

(Sharp-eyed readers may have spotted NotePad lives in the Utilities drawer which is about to get the big heave-ho. Since this chapter is very general, the NotePad will be removed and re-installed. Much the same technique could be applied to another application, say, AmigaBASIC — you might like to try that for yourself.)

Returning to the problem in hand, one simple command can be used to get rid of entire directories in one go — DELETE. Open the Shell and enter these lines (Shell's output is not shown for clarity):

```
1>DELETE Trashcan ALL
1>DELETE Empty ALL
1>DELETE Expansion ALL
1>DELETE Utilities/#?
```

Notice how the Trashcan can easily be removed? Try doing that from the Workbench... You need to leave the Utilities drawer on there because it is accessed during startup, Actually, this isn't strictly necessary but it leaves space to pop other stuff in.

3. Now most of the disk has been cleared out, it is time to remove some of the unwanted items from the System drawer. Enter this:

```
1>DIR System
.info                   CLI
CLI.info                DiskCopy.info
```

```
DiskCopy                FastMemFirst
FastMemFirst.info       Fixfonts
```

[etc.]

There are two entries for every command (Workbench Tool). The name on its own is the command — a program; the name with .info (pronounced dot-info) is the icon file. Icon files are used by the Workbench to store a variety of information, not least the icon's design! There is also an extra dot-info entry — this is created by Workbench when a drawer is opened; and as you might have guessed by now, those dot-info files are just taking up space.

4. The following commands are of no use at this stage: InitPrinter; MergeMem; FixFonts. To get rid of the unwanted files, a slightly different version of the DELETE command is used. However, rather than deleting everything willy-nilly, you just want to select certain names — but to save typing each one whole you can use an AmigaDOS facility called a *wildcard pattern*. For instance, the following removes FixFonts and FixFonts.Info:

```
1>DELETE System/Fix#?
System/FixFonts Deleted
System/FixFonts.Info Deleted
```

In this sense, DELETE looks in the SYSTEM directory with "SYSTEM/" for all the files whose names start with "FIX". By the same method, you can delete the other unwanted files too:

```
1>DELETE System/Mer#?
System/MergeMem Deleted
System/MergeMem.Info Deleted
1>DELETE System/NoF#?
System/NoFastMem Deleted
```

System/NoFastMem.Info Deleted

Lesson 31
Copying an Application

You will need

☞ Your Workbench disk

☞ The disk created in the previous lesson

Surprising as it may seem, even at this stage you still have an almost fully-functioning Workbench disk. Although you cannot change the preferences on that disk, the old ones remain; the Trashcan and some System commands have gone, but the Shell is still active providing some degree of control. In fact, you may find it useful to keep several copies of this disk as ready to run boot disks — because now it's time to put an application on. For this example, I'll use NotePad — but you can boot almost anything from this disk using the methods described.

1. Earlier I used a special trick to make AmigaDOS wait while you got the correct disk ready. For this example I'll use another — based on the RESIDENT command. Enter this:

```
1>RESIDENT C:COPY
```

This makes the COPY command resident in RAM therefore saving a lot of fiddly disk swapping.

2. Now place a copy of the original Workbench disk in the internal drive and enter:

```
1>COPY DF0:Utilities/Note#? to RAM:
DF0:Utilities/NotePad..copied
DF0:Utilities/NotePad.info..copied
```

Used in this way, COPY is directed to find any files in the Utilities directory of the disk in DF0: and make a copy of them in the RAM Disk. Notice that even though the boot Workbench is not present, the command proceeds as normal.

3. Before you do anything else, enter this:

```
1>COPY RAM:Note#? to SYS:
```

When you enter this command AmigaDOS will present a requester asking you to insert the current boot disk; and if you have followed the instructions to date, that will be called BOOT. Insert the disk as requested and proceed to the next step.

Lesson 32
Editing the Startup-Sequence

You will need

☞ Your Workbench disk

☞ The disk created in the previous lesson

The last job is to edit the Amiga's boot startup so NotePad (or whatever application you put on your boot disk) starts when you switch on or reset.

1. Start the ED full-screen editor like this:

```
1>ED S:Startup-sequence
```

2. When ED displays the Startup-sequence, use the cursor keys so the small orange blob — the cursor — is positioned over the L in LoadWB and press Return. This should open a line above LoadWB.

3. Move the Cursor into the empty space and type the name of the application you want to boot on Startup preceded by SYS: —

```
SYS:NotePad
```

in this example.

4. Press the key marked "ESC" (for escape) at the top left of the keyboard. The cursor will now move to the bottom of the screen displaying an asterisk "*". Press X and the Return to save the file.

Important: When making any changes to the Startup-sequence, however slight, always wait for *at least* one second after the disk light goes out before re-setting the machine.

In this part you will have seen there is more to AmigaDOS than meets the casual glance. Do not worry if much of this seems unclear at this stage: you'll soon pixk it up This chapter has only barely scratched the surface of a fascinating subject. There is no easy way to learn AmigaDOS — just hard work and experiment — but the rewards are well worth the effort.

Appendices

A
The Amiga Series

The Amiga A500 may seem nothing special by today's standards; but at its launch less than a decade ago, it represented a giant leap forward. In a market ruled by the PC with its skittish graphics and abominable sound, the Amiga was a tornado of fresh air – even Atari's ST launched at around the same time could not compete.

At grass-roots level the Amiga is a games engine – which accounts for the near-photo quality graphics, fantastic sound and use of customised hardware. But its underlying strength is its ability to multi-task (run several programs at once). Even the lowly A500 can simultaneously: format two disks, download a file from a remote computer, and print a document. And this feature alone has made the Amiga an exhilarating piece of computer hardware – catapulting it so far ahead of the competition, they have never quite caught up.

A1000

This was Amiga's first machine, and long out of production. Although not immensely popular at the time, second-hand examples appear quite frequently. There's nothing overtly wrong with the A1000, but by comparison to the more recent A500 they are not good machines for first-time buyers looking for a bargain. Although the A1000 is an

Amiga at heart, it is only factory fitted with 256K RAM and the printer and serial ports are not standard by accepted PC terms. Few hardware manufacturers support it, making expansion hard to come by and this limits its usefulness. Much the same applies to the early German A2000 which is more or less the same thing. Interestingly, the signatures of the whole design team are extruded on the inside of the case.

A500

This is currently the base machine of the Amiga range – yet that should not be taken as berating it. The A500 is an affordable and expandable micro that will grow as your needs grow. Commodore's latest machine, the CDTV is more or less an A500 with a CD disk drive attached. (Interestingly, some pundits predict Commodore will release a CD drive for the A500 during early 1992 – giving it almost 100 per cent CDTV compatibility.)

Current models are fitted as standard with 512K of RAM in total although Commodore's latest "Cartoon Classics" pack includes a "free" upgrade taking the machine to 1Mb. Whether this policy will continue remains a mystery (certainly Commodore are tight-lipped about it) but it seems a logical progression. Although the official upgrade is via an end-user expansion module, many machines have been shipped with PCBs ready to take the full 1Mb.

Latest rumours imply the 68000 may be surface mounted to the motherboard and this has ramifications for many third-party expansions which rely either on the existing expansion or a socketed CPU to work. Unofficially,

Commodore's stance is simple enough: hardware developers are well aware the machine has provision for external hardware through the 86-pin edge connector located at the right side of the machine.

The A500 is officially sold as a base machine – and users wanting to progress to greater things, such as processor accelerators, should buy at least an A1500 in the first place. Naturally, hardware developers disagree since they see the A500 as being the mass-market machine – something like 90 per cent according to one source. No doubt the debate will carry on long into the night; for the foreseeable future at least, A500s are still an excellent buy.

A1500/2000

These two machines are so closely related some A1500s still have A2000 printed on the rear of the case (sounds of Commodore's marketing bods shooting themselves in both feet abound). In practical terms therefore, there is little to choose between the two. The A1500 is a dual-floppied version of the original machine and the A2000 has been uprated with the addition of a 40Mb hard disk fitted as standard.

This model was a follow-up to the A1000 and continues the modular approach adopted with the original range (although, some would argue, Commodore-Amiga copied the idea from IBM's PC). Whatever the reasoning, the 1500 and 2000 machines take up a fair chunk of desk space and are not suitable for casual home use. More suited to a business environment, these machines can happily take the weight of a monitor and have separate keyboards for ease of access and operator comfort.

The reason for the big box can be summed up in one word – expansion. Unlike the base A500, these models support a slot-based system to which the adventurous can add anything from massive (300Mb plus) hard disks to PC emulators and genlocks. This capability is what makes the 2000 series machines the choice for professional users. Internally fitted hardware occupies no more desktop real-estate than the existing machine and tends to be slightly cheaper than external equivalents. Also, thanks to the perceived market area of the machine, more professional quality hardware is produced for these machines.

A3000/A3000T

These machines are currently Commodore's premier models. Originally launched in two versions (16Mhz and 25Mhz) the slightly cheaper machine has been dropped due to poor sales. All Amiga 3000s are based on Motorola's 68030 CPU – three steps up from the 68000 found in the other models – making them faster and more versatile than their little brothers.

They are also the only machines to feature Commodore's recently updated Workbench and, more significantly, the newest Agnes and Denise chips. This duo, combined with revamped hardware gives the machine an extra graphics mode and a far more versatile Workbench. For example, future software will be able to run in screens that are much larger than can be displayed on a standard monitor – but users can navigate around them just by moving the mouse;

and because the screens actually live in RAM, there will be no sluggish software-based update.

Breaking the mould of the desktop Amigas is the A3000T. A tower based version of the A3000 engine designed to be floor standing. There is also a UNIX based version of the 3000 – often called the 3000UX but this is a developer's only machine and has never been officially released to the public, despite some press reports to the contrary. Remember also, Commodore UK treats its market differently to Commodore US – so just because a machine is "shipping in the States" does not imply it will *ever* get here.

Custom Chips

Although the Amiga range is based on very powerful processors, it is its custom chips which make it so special. These chips, designed to take a load off the CPU freeing it for other tasks, are collectively known as the PAD: Paula, Agnes and Denise. Just to confuse matters, there are other custom chips too like Gary and even a custom keyboard processor! In high-end machines there's Ramsey and (for the sake of giving it a name) Dee. Here's a brief round-up of what they do:

Paula: Custom sound and peripherals support. Responsible for controlling the floppy disk drives and generating the nine octave, four channel stereo sound the Amiga has be praised for.

Agnes: Using the blitter Agnes moves data around memory at mind-numbing speeds – much faster than the 68000 can achieve. It controls graphics, disk and sound DMA and looks after all the system timing from the 28MHz clock. Agnes also controls the Bobs – blitter objects – a type of sprite. Agnes is supplied in three versions depending on the model of machine. Fat Agnes – 512K CHIP RAM (A500); Fatter Agnes – 1Mb CHIP RAM (some A1500/2000s); Super Fat Agnes – 2Mb CHIP RAM (A3000 and A500 Plus).

Denise: Looks after the screen display and all the visuals. Converts images held in RAM to images on a monitor or television. Contains hardware for up to eight sprites. Fat Denise now adds several extra screen modes to later machines such as the A500 Plus and A3000.

Gary: Gate Array. Looks after the bus control signals and address decoding. In addition, Gary helps to drive the floppy disk interface and the keyboard-based reset.

Ramsey: The RAM manager. In conjunction with the 68030's internal MMU, this allows the Amiga 3000 to make the best use of its available RAM.

Dee: The display enhancer. Like Ramsey, this chip is only fitted to the premier A3000 machines. It's used to take the flicker out of interlaced displays.

Copper: Strictly speaking the Copper is part of Fat Agnes. It's a *simple* processor used to control certain functions of the other custom chips. Among other functions, allows the Amiga to provide several different display modes on the same screen. You could therefore have a part of a 4096 colour, low-resolution HAM screen overlapping the four colour, high-resolution Workbench. Although many users take this for granted, no other home micro has this capability.

Feature Check

	A500	A1500/2000	A3000/A3000T
Storage			
Floppy 3,5 880K	1 Internal	1 Internal (2 on A1500)	1 Internal
Floppy 5,25 720K	✪	✢	✪
Hard disk	✢ (20Mb)+	20/40Mb option on A1500	40Mb standard
SCSI interface	✢	Standard	Standard
Tape streamer	✪	✪	✪
Graphics etc.			
Palette colours	4096	4096	4096
Text	80x30 and 60x30	80x30 and 60x30	80x30 and 60x30
Lowest resolution	320 x 200	320 x 200	320 x 200
Colours	16/32/64/4096	16/32/64/4096	16/32/64/4096
Highest resolution	640 x 512 (1)	640 x 512 (1)	1280 x 1024 (1)
Max colours	16	16	16
Anti-flicker	✪	✢	Standard
Sound			
Type	8-bit digital	8-bit digital	8-bit digital
Volume	256 levels	256 levels	256 levels
Range	9 octaves (stereo)	9 octaves (stereo)	9 octaves (stereo)
General			
Workbench	1.3.2	1.3.2	2.0
DOS Supplied	AmigaDOS 1.3.2	AmigaDOS 1.3.2	AmigaDOS 2
OS Supplied	Kickstart 1.3	Kickstart 1.3	Kickstart 2
Processor	68000	68000	68030
68010	✪	✪	-
68020/68881	✪	✢	-
68030/68882	✪	✢	-
Co-processor	✪	✢	Standard 68882
CPU Clock	7.14MHz	7.14MHz	25MHz
Real time clock	✢	Standard	Standard
Power			
Internal PSU	-	200W	200W
External PSU	60W	-	-
Memory			
CHIP (MAX)	512K	512K or 1Mb	1Mb (2Mb)

FAST (MAX)	0Mb (8.5Mb)	0K or 512K (8Mb)	1Mb (16Mb)
Maximum RAM	9Mb	9Mb	18Mb (internal)
ROM	256K	256K	512K
Expansion			
CPU bus	On system bus	1 x 86 pin slot	1 x 86 pin slot
Video bus	None	Yes	Yes
System bus	1 x 86 way edge	5 x 100 pin slots	4 x 100 pin slots
2nd System bus	None	2 x XT/AT slots	2 x XT/AT slots
I/O			
Printer/Parallel	1 x Centronics	1 x Centronics	1 x Centronics
Printer/Serial	Yes (on RS232)	Yes (on RS232)	Yes (on RS232)
RS232	Standard	Standard	Standard
MIDI	✪	✪	✪
Analogue RGB	Standard	Standard	Standard
Digital RGB(I)	Standard	Standard	Standard
Composite video	Standard	Standard	Standard
VGA RGB	No	No	Standard
Analogue to digital	4 – shared with mouse/joystick	4 – shared with mouse/joystick	4 – shared with mouse/joystick
Light pen	☆	☆	☆
Keyboard	94 key internal	94 key external	94 key external
Digital Joystick	☆	☆	☆
Analogue J`stick	☆	☆	☆
Mouse (200 DPI)	Supplied	Supplied	Supplied
Audio out L&R	2 x phono female	2 x phono female	2 x phono female
TV modulator	Standard (external)	✢ (external)	✢ (external)
Price	about £399	£999	£3160

(1) These are standard modes. All machines are capable of *overscanning* the borders, but this is not supported by all software.

☆ Supported in hardware but equipment not supplied as standard.

✪ Accessory/adaptor only available from from independent sources.

✢ Accessory supplied by Commodore and others.

B
The Amiga Buyers Guide

When the Amiga was launched many considered it the most important development in home computer technology since the salad days of Sinclair's ZX series. Sinclair brought home computing to the masses – creating a whole new market with affordable micros based on tried technology. The Amiga, with its designer's radical new ideas, brought forth a computer capable of simultaneously running more than one program at a time within reach of millions; and a new age was born.

Like many of today's computers, the whole Amiga range is in essence very similar. The more you spend, the faster and more powerful the machines become – but all are capable of running the same wide variety of software, and with a few exceptions, the same range of hardware. Indeed, thanks to the massive popularity of the cheaper A500 engine, the choice of peripherals for the basic machine is at least as wide as it is for the higher end models. This can leave the potential buyer in something of a quandary: "Do I save my money and go for an A500 or should I stretch to the A1500?"

Assuming you have an unlimited budget, the choice of machine is limited only by the applications you intend to run. For instance, if you want a machine to just play games the A3000 would be a waste of money. Not only would many titles run too fast, but an equal number will fail given the machine's radically different operating system and architecture. This only affects poorly written software and "metal-bashing" entertainment titles though. Serious applications can expect to find the same environment no matter which machine they happen to be running on: and this is the Amiga's power. Only Apple's Macintosh comes close to the same level of upward compatibility and you have to pay a lot more for the privilege.

This chapter is intended as a guide for those of you who are considering buying a new machine or upgrading an existing one. The main body of the text discusses items of hardware and software with a list of typical examples. The listings are not exhaustive and products mentioned are not necessarily recommended buys.

RAM Expansion

Whichever model you choose, your Amiga will come with at least 512K of RAM – unless you get duped into buying an A1000 – don't. Until recently, all basic machines were fitted with as standard 1/2Mb; higher end models coming with 1, 2 or 4 Mb. Thanks to the popularity of the Amiga, the number of 1Mb A500s in use, and the falling price of RAM, Commodore now looks set to re-specify the A500 with 1Mb. Specialist "trapdoor" expansions such as the KCS PC emulator have been updated to take account of this however.

This possible transition has seen recent packs "including the £99 A501 RAM expansion". Although it could be speculated Commodore is having to dump remaining stocks of its high-quality, but expensive, A501 upgrade in light of many third-party developers offering similar specifications for a quarter of the price or even less! However, you should not buy an expansion which excludes a clock. The saving of around a fiver is not worth it in the long run.

The question of how much memory you actually need is dependent solely on the type of applications you expect to use. However, it should be said, 512K is not really enough for the modern machines and current batch of high powered applications software. This 1/2Mb problem only affects A500 owners but this machine is generally the best supported. For video, graphics and art work 2Mb should be considered absolute minimum – more if you are really serious. And those interested in 3D rendering will have to look for even more. Typical high-powered applications such as Vistapro need 3.5Mb just to run!

One last point worth noting is most internal RAM expansions for the Amiga A500, in addition to being tricky to fit, require a software patch – especially when running under Kickstart 1.2. This can be a bit fiddly to add to every Workbench disk – if in doubt, ask first. This does not affect external RAM boards which will configure themselves correctly at switch on.

Floppy Drives

For anything other than leisure purposes, the single drive supplied with the A500 is a joke. Commodore finally appears to have realised this with the dual-drive standard A1500 – in reality a dual-floppied A2000. The A2000 machines and upward now come with a hard drive fitted as standard. Even so, a second or even third floppy disk drive can be a real boon. Single drive users should consider one essential; hard drive users will discover the need when the time comes to back up that sensitive information.

A500 owners should also note, it is not safe to "daisy-chain" more than one extra drive. The reason usually put forward being the lack of PSU current. However, even though recent advances have seen several high-power PSUs appear, Commodore retains the "two drive only" stance, suggesting more could – in theory – "burn out" the thin tracks on the A500's motherboard. The only solution therefore if you need more than two drives is to go for a unit with its own external power; and the appropriately named, Power Computing is the only company currently making such a drive.

Looking at floppy drives you could be forgiven for thinking there is little to choose between the numerous offerings available. But there is more to the average disk drive than meets the eye. (And for some unfortunate contenders, the wheels of a car in one unmentionable mag Supertest!) During its three to five year life-span, the average floppy drive will have to endure being dropped, washed, bashed, stood on and probably used as a cigarette stand.

Hard Drives

If you think the next best thing to a floppy drive must be a hard one, then you probably have never used one. Hard drives transform the naked and tame little Amiga into a growling beast ready to take on anyone. Hard drives are to disk drives what floppy drives are to 300 baud tape loading systems – remember those? (Even the Spectrum seemed slow at 1500 baud.) As another comparison, you might like to imagine walking from Land's End to John O' Groats and doing the same journey by Concorde. Professional users would not consider a machine that didn't come with a hard disk as standard. With that in mind, here is a rule of thumb: never enter a shop – cheque book in pocket – and casually inquire about a hard drive.

Early Amiga hard drives were crude, slow and on the whole a bit of a slog. I mention these because they are often to be found changing hands on the second-hand market. There's nothing wrong buying a second-hand drive provided you know what you are doing, but overall, newer designs are faster, better specified and more reliable. Something else to bear in mind is if you are still using Kickstart 1.2, hard drives will *not* autoboot – this was added for release 1.3. Also, many older designs – the Commodore's 2090 do not boot from FFS partitions. This latter can cause all sorts of problems if you want to use the FFS.

Another advantage of recent models is most supply some form of RAM expansion. For the A500 this will be in a separate interface box or inside the drive casing itself. The interface-based designs are more convenient to add RAM to, but lose out to the integrated models in terms of styling. Although few designs offer a bus throughport – the majority of other hardware using the expansion bus does supply throughports so this in unlikely to be a source of heartburn. These problem do not haunt the A1500/2000/3000 machines whose drives are usually fitted internally.

Monitors

One of the most important parts of your Amiga system – apart from the CPU itself is the monitor. It might seem a strange revelation to even suggest a good monitor is a vital piece of equipment. Not so. Apart from the keyboard, the monitor is the part of your system through which the machine communicates with you. For every hour you spend at the keyboard your eyes are transfixed on a combination of luminous phosphor and high-frequency radiation. Put another way, the more you spend on a monitor, the more time you can comfortably spend at the machine without risking headaches and eye strain. A good monitor is *essential* for any serious or long term use – from word processing to desktop video.

Monitors come in all shapes and sizes – perhaps the most common being the common, garden or household portable TV. Televisions suffer with a serious problem though – the modulator supplied with the standard A500, although being good for what it is, still degrades the Amiga's excellent video performance. Any Amiga used on a TV should be set for 60 column Workbench and this, frankly, is just not good enough. TV-monitors provide some comfort. Amiga video can sometimes be fed either to the composite or SCART/Peritel video input. This overrides the modulator/de-modulator problem but is still affected by the low-resolution tube found in most domestic sets. If you must use a TV for serious work, use a black and white one – not a colour set with the colour turned down.

A better option would be to plump for a proper monitor with a quoted dot-pitch of around 0.28 (lower numbers are preferred). If the dot-pitch is not specified go for medium resolution. Old CGA (PC) monitors can be pressed into service as can the old BBC favourite, the Microvitec Cub. Better still, the dedicated Commodore unit provides good quality output at an affordable price. The same chassis is also available, badged by original manufacturers, Philips, often at slightly lower cost.

For power users, ie those working with DTP applications, a multi-sync monitor and flicker fixer is the only real choice. The Amiga's display is too small (vertically) to be really useful in standard mode, and the interlaced screen is uncomfortable to use for long stretches. However, such equipment does add to the cost, and is standard on the new high-end Amiga 3000 series machines.

Printers

No matter what sort of serious application you put your machine to, there will come a time when you need to get a hard copy. Whether it be writing a letter to the bank manager, producing a fanzine or producing a work of art – you will need a printer. Printers are probably one of the best-served areas of the microcomputer marketplace because almost all micros have a fairly standard parallel printer port. Even the ones that don't, have a serial adaptor to do the same thing. Given the vast number of PCs in service world-wide, the competition between manufacturers is, to say the least, voracious.

Generally, printers fall into two separate categories – those that use impact methods to produce an image; and those that do not. In each type you will find a wide range of prices and usually a model to suit your needs. Colour printing engines are always more expensive than their mono cousins, and you have to pay a lot to get good quality. Under £1000, colour print engines leave a lot to be desired. The best ones tend to be bubble-jet designs, but these are inherently very expensive to run. Market leaders in the field Canon and Hewlet Packard, both offer high-performance (near-LASER quality) machines priced at under £500 RRP.

Of the impact designs, most users will find a budget nine-pin machine is quite adequate. However, thanks to recent improvements in print-head technology, 24-pin models are now coming increasingly to the fore. For everyday basic printing work, Citizen offer a budget-priced 24-pin machine which costs less than some flashier nine-pin machines! Other manufacturers are hot on Citizen's heels though. Star's much vaunted LC-10 has recently been upgraded and improved to the LC-20 (an LC-10 for the nineties, say Star). They also offer the cost effective mono/colour LC-200 design, which, although a little slow offers good overall performance for the money.

Note: most dealers now supply a lead as part of the asking price. If you have an A1000 or A2000 (not B2000) you *must* get a special (25 way D female) lead.

Modems

The term modem is a contraction of two words: Modulator and De-modulator. Modems (there's a lot of them around) are used to connect computers together over vast distances via a telephone line. Modems give you access to a vast amount of information, from the sublime to the ridiculous; you can even get "on-line" to your favourite authors via CIX and play interactive games (*games*?) with real people. Through the vast number of bulletin board system (BBSs), you can access megabytes of PD and Shareware software – the list of uses is almost endless. There is one thing for certain, the world of computer communications (experts call it comms) is a bug which you are unlikely to shake easily. (However, like the infamous 0898 numbers, remember to check with whoever pays the phone bill before logging on!)

Like most computer equipment, with modems you get what you pay for. Modem speeds are often quoted using the V codes such as V21/V23 or V22bis. Respectively, these mean 1200 baud (in)/75 baud (out), 300 and 2400 baud – both ways. As you pay more you will be able to achieve speeds in excess of 9600 baud (fast) with error correction and real-time data compression! Whatever you do, unless the budget is really restrictive go for an intelligent modem (look for words such as Hayes or AT command compatible) and you should be on the right road.

➠ Beware of cheap US imports. Not only do these usually come with the wrong type of telephone plug, it is illegal to connect them to any BT, Mercury or Hull City Council telephone equipment. Such equipment should carry a red warning triangle "Prohibited for use with equipment operated by British Telecom..." but not everything does. Approved equipment, has a green circle attached.

Accelerators

Not a lot of people know this [FX: *uuuurgh*], but the Amiga is actually quite a fast machine. Why on earth then would you want to speed it up even more? The need for more speed has been an obsession with computer fiends since before the pocket calculator. If someone brings out a fast machine, you can almost guarantee within six months someone will have produced a quicker one. This has been aided by Motorola constantly reducing the price of the 68000 chips and developing faster ones. Currently, bank account allowing, you can get a 68040 running at 50MHz – effectively, something like 15 times faster than the standard A500!

The crunch comes when you try to choose from the barrage of technical specifications thrown at you: "25MHz, 68881, 32-bit RAM". There are two important factors.

1: The actual processor used. The 68000 can only execute instructions at a given speed, so by doubling the clock frequency you will barely notice the difference. The 68010 is a little better. With its small (two word) instruction prefetch certain data transfer loops speed up a little. The improvement for most software is likely to be under ten per cent though. The 68020 has a 256 byte instruction cache whereas the 30 and 40 have data caches as well. Forget what that means: in real terms, the speed increase for these beasties can be 100 per cent or even more at any given clock rate!

2: Whether or not a maths co-processor is installed. These clever devices do all the hard floating-point mathematics for the CPU – and therefore, for your software. Since these dedicated chips, which rival the CPU in complexity, are very good at mathematics they can speed up maths intensive applications (spreadsheets, ray-tracing etc.) several hundred fold; but *only* if the software supports them. It's no good lashing out over 100 quid on a 68882, if your spreadsheet still insists on handling the maths itself.

Music Hardware

If you have a penchant for music, you will find the Amiga's sound – and good range of free music software – a real bonus. Although the machine has been around for some years now, there is still little to touch it soundwise. Moreover, recent developments in software have seen the four channel hardware limit pushed to eight channels: up to four different synthesized instruments playing simultaneously in each stereo channel.

Not only that, but thanks to electronic sampling each *instrument*, could easily be anything from an acoustic guitar to Luciano Pavarotti, to an entire symphonic chorus. Budding Bachs and Beethovens should have plenty to satisfy them there. And MIDI freaks will be pleased to see the range of high quality MIDI interfaces ready and waiting to hook up to their keyboards – living proof the Amiga is still probably the most versatile micro you can buy. (The software is covered later.)

Video Presentation

The Amiga is known for its graphics. However, not everyone knows it has built-in support for genlock (video mixing) hardware – and this has opened the doors for a whole host of them From the casual Camcorder user, to the semi-professional video production agency, to a broadcast studio, there is a Genlock to suit *your* needs. Indeed the Amiga has been used by independent television companies for a number of years now.

At the other end of video, there are a variety of frame grabbers – little back boxes for pinching images from moving video and digitizing them in all their glory. Typically such images can be used as they are, or re-touched and used in demos and animations.

For those with money to burn, (and the patience for it to arrive) there is New Tek's long-awaited video toaster. A system for producing professional video effects, fades, blurs, wipes – you name it. Although still not available in the UK, it has already amassed more interest than the machine that spawned it – the Amiga itself. Meanwhile over in the US, manufacturer New Tek, is rumoured to be selling Toasters faster than it can make them.

Emulators

Ask yourself this: why on earth would you want your shiny new Amiga to imitate a different machine? You bought the thing in the first place for its acclaimed graphics, sound and usability – so why spend money making it behave like a tinny little 8-bit PC? The answer is software; because there are something in excess of one million titles for the PC alone. Different machines have their own strengths too – the Mac is known for DTP, the BBC for education; the PC for business and so on.

There are a wide variety of emulations from pure hardware to pure software; with some in between. Typically, the hardware emulators are more expensive but work better and faster because the software is running on a *real* machine – not a virtual one emulated in software. One exception to this rule is Commodore's BBC Emulator, which runs BBC BASIC at something like seven times the speed of the original 2MHz BBC model B. Some emulators, such as A-Max tread a fine line between the legal and the illegal – because the original manufacturer, Apple in this case, jealously guards its copyright. (Rightly too, in my opinion.)

It seems unlikely such problems will be resolved in the foreseeable future. Until then you can enjoy the benefits of a wide range of machines from Spectrums to STs. The list presented contains just a few of those currently on offer.

Productivity

Productivity software is an all-encompassing term surrounding a variety of software aimed mainly at business and serious home users. It covers anything from word processors, through databases and spreadsheets, to home accountancy packages. The four major categories are as follows:

Word processing

This software is designed to help you make the most of your writing skills, and, in some cases, enhance them. In their simplest (and cheapest) form, word processors allow you to enter, edit and format text before finally committing to paper. This is a great improvement over the humble typewriter because you get a chance to review and correct the text – without the need for voluminous amounts of correction fluid.

Better word processors include a variety of tools such as spelling checkers; thesauri and mail merging – so you can easily send the same letter to several people. One even has its own database (see below)! As cost and power increases you get into the realms of document publishers – sometimes confusingly called word publishers. These are just word processors with the capability to import graphics and process text, often containing a variety of styles and type-faces, very precisely. Such things are a bridge between simple word processors and full-blown typesetting systems – and are usually more than adequate for casual use such as newsletters etc.

Databases

In computer terms, databases are a fairly recent innovation – but many users would be lost without them. The world without databases would be a world without direct (junk) mail: *ah, bliss*. Typically, databases hold information. Any information – whether it be a list of names and addresses, to 20 years of football league results, to population statistics.

Simple (flat-file) databases will allow you to store simple data and retrieve or print it in list form. Normally some form of search facility is provided to located data easily. In any case, they certainly beat file cards! More powerful systems allow data to be stored and accessed in an increasing number of ways.

Relational systems allow one set of data to access other sets of data, automatically and updating links as it goes. This might be used to hold a list of the products offered by different suppliers. One set of data – the addresses – remains fairly static. The other may be in constant flux; and in any case each supplier could have hundreds of different items. Using a relational system, the data can be cross-referenced (item to supplier) quickly, easily and without having to store the same details many times over.

Spreadsheets

Spreadsheets are mathematical toys; open-ended applications intended to allow the end-user to define their own application. If that sounds a little mind-boggling – then just consider many spreadsheets can double as accounts systems, databases and even word processors. Spreadsheets are not for everyone – because unless you have some idea of what you want from them, they're as useful as chocolate fireguards.

Every blank spreadsheet is a program waiting to be written. Each cell – many sheets have thousands – is like a powerful pocket calculator in its own right. Now imagine being able to connect all the results together and compile results or draw tables. Many sheets run programs either automatically on startup or by user action.

They can be used for almost any application which requires handling large numbers of figures. From cashflows and profit and loss projections to statistical analysis and forecasting. Without a doubt, spreadsheets are one of the most fascinating and useful of all the productivity software. But that power comes at a price – ease of use.

Integrated

These packages are bundles of useful software available for less than the cost of buying each package separately. Typically, they will include a database, spreadsheet and word processor – but may have others not available elsewhere. Gold Disk's office includes Page Setter for instance. The advantage of integrated systems is the software involved can swap data easily. This makes labourious tasks such as mail-merging much easier. On the down side, you will find some applications are not as good as others. Analyse for instance, is a perfectly capable spreadsheet in The Works Platinum pack, but is let down somewhat by the Scribble word processor. In any event, integrated systems can be a very good starting point; either for those on a tight budget or folk who do not know which applications they require.

Financial

Costing and invoicing systems are tailor made for home users and small businesses to help them keep track of the tricky side of business – figures. These programs cover a variety of topics from stock control and invoicing through VAT and tax returns. One point worth mentioning here, if you are using a computer to calculate VAT or income tax for a business you must inform the relevant government department. Although the better databases spreadsheets can be programmed to do most of the functions covered here, in many cases a custom application will do it better. In any case, if you need a VAT package, *make sure* it has been approved by HM Customs and Excise before you start using it. If not, you could find yourself in hot water.

DTP

There are currently only two widely used DTP packages for the Amiga – although some of the more powerful word processors offer at least some DTP facilities. Of those – PageStream 2.1 and Pro Page 2.0 – each has its followers, but Gold Disk's Pro Page seems to be gaining ground in many circles. Certainly it's the preferred choice of many DTP experts. No doubt the battle between the two companies will rage for some time yet. (Thanks to A-Max, those with money to burn – could ignore these completely and buy the Macintosh system, Quark Express 3.0 – the very program used to produce many news-stand magazines!)

Although Page Stream and Pro Page are totally incompatible, both can take advantage of the variety of support products such as extra fonts and clip art – so no one gets left out. Also included in this section are some scanners – useful tools for anyone with more than a passing interest in DTP.

Music Software

Admittedly, this is not my specialist area – but judging from the sounds often to be heard coming from next door, the Amiga is as versatile in this area as it is in many others. Music systems fall into two major categories: trackers and notational composers. Trackers are simpler – each note is represented by a series of numbers – duration, frequency, volume, instrument and so on. At first glance trackers look horrendously complex – but in truth they are very simple once mastered.

Conversely, notational composers are tools for accomplished musicians and anyone with a burning desire to learn music. Songs are composed on staves where each note is shown as it would be on real sheet music. Remember though, although most systems only *play* four channels at once, each note can be any instrument – so songs entire symphonies can be produced; if you have the patience. Recent offerings like OctaMED can combine the two and play eight channels at once. And for the price, OctaMED is a great introduction.

Most Amiga systems incorporate a MIDI sequencer of some sort which can record and play up to 16 channels on any number of different MIDI instruments. The operating limitations are determined by the hardware of course, which usually has to be bought separately.

Art Packages

There is little doubt when it comes to graphics few systems can rival the Amiga's versatility. Although other systems boast larger palettes and better resolutions, none come close at the price. Furthermore, the Amiga's accepted standard graphics format, IFF, has meant a high degree of compatibility between art systems from a variety of developers. In effect, the user with money to burn can use the best facilities from a range of graphics tools without having to fiddle with an endless stream of conversion utilities.

Art packages are most often used for leisure purposes – but they can just as easily re-touch images from digitisers and frame grabbers. Software authors use them too – developing everything from sprites to backdrops for graphical user interfaces. Thanks to the power of the machine and the quality of the software – even children can become accomplished artists with the wide range of tools provided. Photon Paint 2 for instance has a surface mapping feature where a picture can be wrapped onto 3D shapes and more besides; Digi-Paint 3 can colourize monochrome images; Deluxe Paint 4 has advanced animation facilities and supports a wide range of screen modes too.

Video

Right, so you've shot your video of the best man tripping over a drunken usher, cannoning into the bride who decimates the five-tier wedding cake; and you want to add the odd caption or two. Video titling has never been easier

– all you need are two videos (one from next door perhaps) an Amiga, genlock, and the software to mix it all up. Basic titles can be added with a bit of imagination and a good paint package – say Deluxe Paint – but for those really fancy wipes, fades, blurs and that professional *feel* custom-built software is the only solution.

Strangely enough, although there seems to be a large number of genlocks on sale, the amount of software is surprisingly small. Don't let that put you off however – because as always the quality is pretty good. Top of the league (for the moment) is Scala: 17 fonts; scrolling titles; 59 backgrounds; over 70 transitions and an animation player too- "yer gets what yer pays for". For occasional use though there's always Home Titler. While for the semi-pro with an interest in the technical side, ZVP produce a system tailored for professionals which has a selection of clocks and other video sundries.

Languages

In bygone days when 8-bits ruled the roost, one of the most popular leisure pursuits – rivalling games – was writing programs. In those days, virtually every home micro came with a version of the BASIC language built into ROM. (One exception being the Jupiter Ace, which came with FORTH instead.) Prior to that, BASIC had to be booted from tape, a long and arduous process. Things have come a long way since, but the 16-bits have returned to the old system where the machine comes fitted with a basic operating system and precious little else; BASIC, once again, has gone back to mass-media – disk in this case.

All this might seem like a throwback – but it opens doors for a wide variety of other programming languages and even different versions of BASIC. For accomplished and potential programmers alike this opens new doors -from writing a simple applications to vast new games – there is a language suitable. Be cautious when it comes to reading the packaging and adverts though. Just as any programming language takes time to learn, any program takes to time write. It's no use getting Europress Software's AMOS BASIC and expecting to write a best seller in two weeks if you have no idea what PRINT means. Most mainstream languages have a version in the Public Domain – so if you want try something weird and wonderful, try there first.

Widgets

Typically these are the sort of little gadgets and stocking fillers you can ask your favourite aunty for when Christmas comes around. (Whoops, there I go getting all commercial.) There are literally dozens of gadgets and extras: replacement mice; optical mice; cordless mice and joysticks; mouse mats; external cases; keyboard protectors; fancy disk labels... and so it goes on. For rich aunties, you might even consider asking for 24-bit graphics card? You'll find these goodies – and more -lurking among the advertiser's listings in most Amiga magazines.

Free Software!

Welcome to the wonderful world of Amiga Public Domain. Here you'll find literally thousands of pieces of software just there for the taking — and most of it doesn't cost a bean. Public Domain (PD) software is there for all of us to enjoy and covers just about everything from games to "serious" applications. Sounds almost too good to be true? In truth PD is rarely as straightforward as "software for the taking."

Public Domain: True Public Domain software has no copyright attached to it. This means the author has given up all his rights to copyright under international law. This form of PD in the purest sense is very rare indeed and the term has become almost generic with Freeware. PD Software can be given to anyone by anyone. It was written by someone who has decided to share it with like-minded others at no cost to anyone.

Freeware: This is just like PD software, but the author has retained the copyright. In practice the difference between PD and Freeware is almost inconsequential. Authors of Freeware software retain all international copyright to their product, but allow users to pass it amongst themselves.

Shareware: This is not like PD or Freeware and is a concept developed in America. Here you get a fully working version of the program which you can use for a fixed amount of time — 30 days usually. After that time you must pay the author a registration fee or destroy all copies. Even if you decide not to keep it, you will be encouraged to pass Shareware software on to your friends.

Charityware: Works the same way as Shareware, but instead of paying the authors you make a donation to a registered charity. You must do this or you will be infringing the copyright law — and this carries a severe fine or even imprisonment. Of Charityware one insider said, "Some day all [PD] software will be sold this way."

Licenceware: This works rather like Shareware, only the authors get more protection from thieves. [Yes, thieves. This is no time for using euphemisms like Pirates.] These products are distributed by licensed libraries for a fixed fee. Part of the fee is then passed back to the author — a franchised sale, if you like. Licenceware and Shareware titles alike, are usually very cost- effective compared with commercial offerings and often better quality than the Freeware examples.

Catch — It's Free

It is said, "there's no such thing as a free lunch." and this is true, here are the catches.

➡ You cannot usually nip down to the shop and buy a whole load of PD software because the shops are not allowed to make a profit by selling it. In fact, many authors specifically preclude shops from even giving their software away as an incentive to buy the machine. This is their right and after all, they wrote the program to help other users, not to line the pockets of some salesman!

➠ PD software is usually only distributed by special “PD libraries” although you may be able to pick it up from friends and your local user group. The catch with this is you don’t know what you are going to get before it arrives. You will be able to get a guide to what’s best from more informed magazines which include special “PD” sections. Watch out you don’t get charged too heavily. Some libraries charge over three quid for a PD disk — which is getting rather high — so shop around for a good deal. At this price you should get a disk full of software, not just one or two small programs.

➠ Most PD programs are written by programmers for other programmers. Therefore with a PD product the manual will usually be limited and come on disk. Some programs don’t even go this far; a lot need some knowledge of the CLI. On the up side, with a bit of work, PD is a great way to find out what the machine can do. Some user groups produce PD demo disks which can be booted just like a game. Shareware and Licenceware products are better and when you register some authors will send a printed manual. As long as you don’t expect a professionally typeset and bound tome, you won’t go far wrong.

C
Where to Buy

Getting the best system for your needs is easy; the hard part is sourcing the components at a price you can afford. One of the main aims of this section is to help you do just that. However, you should always let your fingers do the walking and be prepared to do a little research for yourself before finally parting with cash.

The advertisers in most good magazines are all reputable firms, but each has its own speciality. For instance, if you are looking for a new floppy disk it would be inadvisable to call software specialists. Similarly, if it's software you are after, then a hardware specialist is unlikely to be able to give you a good deal.

This is not always true of course, many items of hardware also require support software. Sound samplers, MIDI interfaces and genlocks are three typical instances. Most dealers will bundle some form of software with such hardware – but in many cases a better package may well be available separately. In these cases you may find the hardware specialist will be able to give you a better deal – but often only at "point of sale". And be prepared to haggle. Although the margins on hardware are not good, many dealers value the custom in this uncertain trade, so don't be afraid to negotiate; this applies in particular to software bundled with hardware.

Finally, watch out for grey imports. Although not illegal, some suppliers have been known to supply US versions of hard and software. This can be troublesome in two ways. First, if you need technical support, grey importers (sometimes called "box shifters" in the trade although the two are not always the same) will rarely be in a position to help. Moreover, if you register US software from the UK, the originating software house is unlikely to be willing to give helpline support and upgrades. Reputable dealers will be able to help and advise – although you may have to pay a little more for the privilege.

Even if you have enough expertise to manage on your own, some US releases are intended for use on an NTSC screen and will be unable to make the best use of the extra 50 or so lines available with PAL. This problem extends to certain items of video hardware, which will either deliver poor performance, or worse, refuse to work at all!

The Exhibition Circuit

In just about every month of the year, somewhere, someone is having a computer show. The past few years have seen an upsurge then sudden decline, but they're on the increase once more. Briefly, shows split into three groups:

All Comers Shows

There are several of these, typically: The 16-bit Show, The Computer Shopper Show and the Personal Computer Show (previously known as PCW). The organisers of the PC Show will be mortified to see themselves grouped here because theirs is aimed at a more serious market, viz IBM and friends.

The user shows "Shopper" and "16-bit" are useful for picking up bargains. Anything general: a new printer ribbon, to an anti-glare monitor screen, to a cuddly mouse cover — you name it. These shows are full of little and large dealers selling all sorts, for all sorts! The Personal Computer show is something of a dead duck for most Amiga owners — it may be worth a visit if you have nothing better to do.

Dedicated Shows

The Commodore Show (now known as World of Commodore) is the main event for Amiga owners. Over the last few years, it could have almost have been called the Amiga show. Although Commodore market their own PC range and the hugely successful C64 machine, most exhibitors seem a bit reticent to support them. Now located at the Earl's Court in London, the World of Commodore Show splits into two halves: the mail-order dealers and the more serious companies. It's the place to see the people that make the world of Amiga tick, point fingers, take pictures, and perhaps throw them a few nuts. It is also the best place to go if you need straight talking, impartial advice from the experts.

Because this is a dedicated show, organised on behalf of Commodore, you will be able to check out the new equipment for yourself. Even to the extent of viewing brand new machines like the CDTV or the A1500. You'll get hands on experience of the Amiga 3000 and see the

Amazing Workbench 2 in all its glory at 25MHz. Typically this show attracts a very wide audience. Exhibitors try to show off their new games, hardware and software and you get crushed in the aisles.

If you want to get down to some serious talking with suppliers and get chance to try out expensive hardware, go on the first public day. On the other hand, if you want to get a bargain at one of these shows, go on the last day with a bundle of cash and make offers in the last hour before closing. In either case, there is little point getting there very early. If you get there two or three hours after the show has opened its doors, you will be able to get in without having to queue for hours.

Specialist Shows

There are a few of these spattered around the calendar, few are of any interest. You may find the Computer Graphics Show, The BETT (education) and even the Robot Olympics worth a trek. These exhibitions are not dedicated to the Amiga but because of the machine's potential in these areas, it does feature heavily.

The Dealers

If you go to a specialist computer dealer, you will have to pay the full recommended retail price for your machine; more in some cases. If, on the other hand, you go to a typical high-street retailer you will invariably pay slightly less. Now ask yourself, why?

The major outlets can buy machines in bulk, negotiate better deals with Commodore, and sell them at lower cost. But because they are located in primary sites they also have higher overheads rent etc. — and that eats into profit. Let's call this a hidden cost.

When you buy a machine, you go for the best deal — but is the best deal necessarily the cheapest? The crunch comes when you turn to your dealer for support. Although the situation has improved over the last few years it is still far from perfect. The National Association of Specialist Computer Retailers (N.A.S.C.R) say of chain stores, "Again, fine if you know exactly what you want and don't want any technical back up or assistance, because if you return with a query or problem you may just find you have more knowledge than the person that sold it to you!"

Responding to this, a spokesperson for the Dixons group who have specialist "Business Centres" in more than 80 of their branches had this to say, "Our customers can get expert help and advice... Because all staff are put through an intensive training course, we would expect our staff to be able to help people."

Support can be viewed in two ways:

Hard and Software Sales

Most of you will quickly outgrow the packages bundled with the machine. Skimming through the pages of a magazine, you discover the package which seems to meet your needs, and nip to the shop, only to be greeted by "Sorry sir, we don't sell that" or worse "Database? What's a database?" Your only recourse is either get it mail order or look for a local specialist. Inevitably this will be the tiny independent retailer tucked away in a back street somewhere, whose shelves resemble Aladdin's cave.

If you bought a "vanilla" Amiga A500 you'll need to expand the machine very quickly unless you just want to play games. But what do you need first? How much does it cost? Where can you get it? The buyers guide should help answer most of those questions, but in a nutshell, the simple answer is forget the major high-street chains and go back to a specialist. These people form the backbone of the computer industry — without them, the industry would not exist.

Technical help

If there's one thing you can say about salesmen, they're great at selling things. As soon as you cross the threshold they descend on you like vultures to a fresh corpse. Getting rid of them is just as easy though, you just have to know the magic words: "I seem to be having some trouble with my machine..." Nine times out of ten you won't even make it past the "t" in "trouble" when poof, they vanish faster than the turkey on Christmas Day. Some of them leave skid marks.

The official word from Commodore if you have a problem with your machine — whether it be hard or software — is go back to your supplier. At present the company does not have a technical help desk for the general public, instead they expect their dealers to deal with simple queries themselves. Official Commodore dealers should be able to deal with most problems on the spot and otherwise can contact the company on your behalf.

According to Commodore one of the most common problems people experience with the Amiga is getting it to work with their printer. This is a relatively basic requirement if you are going to get the best from your machine, however, few non-specialist dealers are able to answer this problem.

Should large chains be allowed to sell the Amiga or should it be restricted to specialists? This question has been argued many times but the simple answer is, yes. Large dealers must be allowed to sell at least the Amiga otherwise it will be perceived as a “snobbish” business micro. Apple has adopted the policy of licensed dealerships for the Macintosh range because it’s a specialist machine targeted at a specific business market. The home market is a whole new ball-game where everyone plays by different rules. Caveat emptor — QED!

Returning Faulty Hardware

Good salesmen are not a protected species — but they ought to be. As an ex-shop assistant, this author can speak from personal experience: if there’s one thing worse than a customer who knows his rights; it’s the one who thinks he does. The one who knows his rights will get what he wants very quickly; the one who thinks he does will argue the sky is pink and get nowhere fast.

If you think your Amiga is faulty and want to return it, you must be able to prove it fails to meet with one of the following statements:

① It must be of merchantable quality

② As described

③ It must be fit for the purpose for which it was sold

Whoever wrote those rules could have written as a PS, “Abandon hope all ye who try to prove them.”

In simple terms, if any of those three — apparently straightforward rules — has been broken you *may* be able to

➠ Return it for a refund

OR

➠ Get compensation for part of the value

OR

➠ Get a replacement/free repair

It gets sticky from here, because the onus is on YOU to prove which of the three rules has been breached. You must also do so within a reasonable period. The precise timing is not defined in law, but after the machine is more than a week or two old, things start to get awkward. Age is defined as being the period elapsed between date of purchase and the date the fault was reported. For this reason, you must report any problems to your supplier as soon as you discover them.

This affects Christmas buyers worst, because if the machine was bought as a present some weeks previously, it can be considered as aged goods. That is: outside the period for refund or replacement. Most reputable dealers will offer to replace a machine that was obviously faulty on its date of sale without question. Remember though, they don't legally have to! You cannot return something if you decide you didn't want it after all.

If You Have To Return a Machine

- ✓ Keep calm: Losing your temper will only make matters worse.
- ✓ Take some proof of purchase: If the machine was bought as a present you may have to get the buyer to return the goods for you.
- ✓ Make sure you're right about the fault: Beginners often mistake features of a machines operation as fault.
- ✓ Consult an independent expert: This should save the embarrassment of having to admit you were to blame.
- ✓ If you bought the machine on credit (credit card, HP etc.) you may be able to take action against the credit company. This applies *even if* the original seller has gone bust or just refuses to help. For this reason, if you buy goods at an exhibition, it's usually better to use a credit card if you have one.

Returning Software

If taking a faulty machine back was tricky this is worse. Software is a very subjective purchase — especially with all the copying going on — few dealers will do anything except replace software with the same title. Before wasting a trip to the shop, try to decide if the software is at fault — here are those rules again, applied to software.

- If the disk boots and the manual and packaging are in good condition, then it could be deemed as being of merchantable quality.
- If the package does everything it claims to — no matter how slowly or clumsily — then it works as described.
- This is the awkward one: games must be playable and programming languages must be capable of producing a program — that's all. Just because you can't complete Level I of "Asterod Meets The Terrapin Bashers" does not mean the game was not fit for the purpose, it just means it was too hard for you. Similarly, just because you can't write a best selling arcade game in AMOS doesn't mean there is something wrong with AMOS — it just reflects on you. The only recourse you have in this case, is from the second rule — and most software houses are wise enough not to make too many extravagant claims.

The guidelines given here have been adapted from an interview with a Consumer Advice Centre and from The Office of Fair Trading's leaflet, "How to put things right." Some of the rights discussed may differ slightly in Scotland, Northern Ireland and other countries; contact an independent adviser first.

Quick Buyer's Reference

A500 RAM Expansions

Size	Price	Notes
512K	£20-40	Easily fitted underneath machine
1.5Mb	£79	Internal — will invalidate warranty
2Mb	£105	Internal — will invalidate warranty
1Mb	£130	External/FAST
8Mb	£519	External FAST
4Mb	£249	Internal/FAST

A1500/2000/3000 RAM Expansions

Size	Price	Notes
2Mb	£200	A1500/A2000
2Mb	£199	A1500/A2000
4Mb	£275	A1500/A2000
8Mb	£345	A1500/A2000
8Mb	£449	A1500/A2000
1Mb FAST RAM	£109	A3000 only
4Mb	£500	A3000 only

Floppy Disk Drives and Sundries

Model	Price	Notes
PC880	£55	Good value drive with anti-click
PC880B	£65	Blitz copier, anti-click, anti-virus
RF332C	£45	Basic but cheap
Roclite	£65	Very slim drive — available in black
Internal 500	£49	Replaces DF0:
Internal 2000	£50	Fits as DF0: or DF1:
PC880B2	£110	Twin version on PC880
Roc Knight	£20	Advanced anti-virus and track display.
Boot selector	£17	Internal fitting

Drive Switch One	£11	Drive disable for DF1:
DOS-2-DOS	£30	Read PC formatted disks

A500 Hard Disks and Sundries

Model	Price	Capacity	Max. RAM
Supra 500XP	£489	40Mb	8Mb
A590	£299	20Mb	2Mb
A590 52Mb	£490	52Mb	2Mb
A590 105Mb	£640	105Mb	2Mb
ICD Novia 30i	£399	20Mb	NA
ICD Prima 105	£499	42Mb	NA
Protar HD	£299 up	20Mb up	8Mb
GVP Impact II+	£699	100Mb	8Mb
Syquest	£780	88Mb	0Mb
Sankyo tape	£690	150Mb	NA

A2000 Hard Disks and Sundries

Model	Price	Capacity	Max. fitted RAM
A2901-40	£200	40Mb	0Mb
Nexus HC	£349	40Mb	8Mb
Series II HC+8	£549	114Mb	8Mb
Series II HC+8	£369	40Mb	8Mb
Wordsync 2000	£449	40Mb	0Mb
Syquest removable	£690	88Mb	0Mb
Sankyo streamer	£600	150Mb	NA

Amiga Monitors and Accessories

	Price	Notes
Philips TVM	£270	Basically a TV — with Teletext!
CBM 1084S	£260	Philips engine with CBM badging
Mutiscan	£330	0.28 dot-pitch
Philips 8833-II	£320	Philips own cased version of 1084S
Flicker Free	£250	A500 compatible

A1950	£450	Multi-sync monitor
A2320	£220	Flicker fixer for A1500/A2000 models
Flicker Fixer	£150	A2000 only

Parallel Printers

	Price	Type	Notes
Citizen 120D+	£150	Impact	Budget 9 pin
Epson LX-850	£270	Impact	9 pin
Citizen124D	£290	Impact	Cheap 24 pin
CitizenSwift 9	£275	Impact	Colour option
Star LC-200	£300	Impact	Colour/mono
CitizenSwift 24	£430	Impact	Super 24 pin
HP Deskjet 500	£400	Inkjet	Sheet feeder inc.
Canon BJ-10e	£260	Inkjet	mono only
Canon BJ-330	£500	Inkjet	300DPI mono

Modems

	Price	Max Baud	MNP	Notes
Pace Linnet	£230	1200	No	Approved by BABT
Pace Linnet	£300	2400	No	Approved by BABT
Supra 2400	£150	2400	No	External
Supra 2400zi	£120	2400	No	A1500/2000 only
Falcom 2400	£406	2400/9600	Level 5	Approved by BABT
Supra 2400 +	£200	2400/9600	Level 5	External
Supra 2400 zi+	£170	2400/9600	Level 5	A1500/2000 only

Accelerator Cards

	Price	MHz/Pro/Co	RAM spec.	Machines
A2030	£1000	25/30/68882	2Mbx32bit	A2000
HARMS Pro30	£1100	28/30/68882	4Mbx32bit	A2000
GVP 3001	£2200	50/30/68882	4Mbx32bit	A2000
B5000	£595	25/20/68881	1Mbx32bit	A500
B5000	£1162	40/30/68882	4Mbx32bit	A500/A2000
VXL30	from £316	25/30/option	optional	A500/2000

VXL30	£1289	40/30/68882	4Mbx32bit	A500/2000
CSA MMR	from £390	33/30/68882	up to 8Mb	A500
HARMS 020	from £150	8/20/68881	None	A500/2000

Music hardware

	Price	Type
Mini Midi	£30	Microscopic MIDI adaptor
Midi Interface 2	£30	Versatile MIDI adaptor
Sound Trap 3	£30	Mini mono sampler and pass-thru
AMAS	£100	Sampler with integral MIDI
Stereo Sampler II	£40	High-speed stereo sampler
Audio Engineer +	£199	Probably the best sampler around
MiniAmp	£40	5W per channel — speakers extra
ZyFi	£40	Ampified speaker system
Sound Enhancer	£35	Improves high-frequency sound

Video Hardware

	Price	Type
Colourpic	£400	Real-time frame grabber
Digi View Gold	£150	Still-frame colour digitiser
Rocgen	£115	Basic genlock with fade facility
Rocgen Plus	£190	New genlock with mask and faders
Superpic	£500	Better Colourpic, with a genlock!
Video Toaster	$1600	Better than sliced bread? NTSC only
VideoCentre	£760	Super-duper studio genlock
VideoCentre Plus	£1170	As above with extra fades etc.

Emulators

	Price	Emulates	RAM Modes	Machines
Powerboard	£235	IBM PC-XT	720K + 192K	A500
AT-Once	£199	IBM PC-AT	720K + >7Mb	A500/A2000
XT Bridgecard	£199	IBM PC-XT	512K	A2000
AT Bridgecard	£799	IBM PC-AT	1Mb	A2000

Chameleon	£30	Atari ST	512K	A500/A2000
Spectrum	£3	Spectrum 48	na	All models
QL Emulator	£3	Sinclair QL	na	All models
CP/M Emulator	£3	CP/M 2.2	64K	All models
A-Max	£250	Mac SE	na	A500/A2000
The Emulator	£40	BBC B+	64K	All models

Word and Document Processors

	Price	Notes
Scribble	£30	Crude but simple word processor
Transwrite	£50	Fast and efficient word processor
Pen Pal	£80	DP with internal database!
Kind Words 2	£50	Early DP — sloooow....
Excellence	£130	DP with loads of featues
Protext 4.2	£100	Standard text machine
Protext 5.5	£155	Adds thesaurus, RTF etc. to 4.2
Wordworth	£130	Highly acclaimed document machine

Database packages

	Price	Notes
Infofile	£50	Cheap flat-file system
Prodata 1.2	£100	Sister to Protext — slow
Superbase Personal	£30	Cheap and powerful — but hard to get
Superbase Personal 2	£100	Very powerful...
Superbase Pro 4	£412	Most powerful around

Spreadsheets

	Price	Notes
Superplan	£80	Powerful but slow
Analyse	£50	Cheap and easy!
Maxiplan 500	NA	Powerful, if bugged
Advantage 1.1	£100	Highly acclaimed
K-Spread 3	£70	GEM lookalike
K-Spread 4	£100	Powerful but ugly

Financial

	Price	Notes
Cashbook Controller	£50	Adequate for small business use
Home Accounts	£30	Ideal toy for big spenders
System 3	£50	Stock control/invoicing
System 3 Enhanced	£70	Bigger version of System 3
Personal Finance Man	£30	Rival to Cashbook Controller
Personal Tax Planner	£40	Keep the Inland Revenue happy
Final Accounts	£30	P&L, balance sheets, A/C ratios

Integrated Systems

	Price	Notes
Publisher's Choice	NA	WP, Spreadsheet, database
Gold Disk Office	£130	Advantage, transwrite etc.
The Works Platinum	£90	Scribble2, Analyse2 etc.

DTP Software and Sundries

	Price	Notes
Page Setter 2	£62	Basic system — stripped Pro Page
Page Stream 2.1	£205	Power DTP — part 1
Pro Page 2.0	£130	Power DTP — part 2
Saxon Publisher	£270	New entry — the new top dog?
Saxon Script	£100	Adobe Postscript interpreter
Outline Fonts	£135	Extra fonts for Pro Page/PageStream
Pictureware	£5 each	Superb library of digitised photos
Pro Clips	£25	Selection of clip art
Clip Art Library	£20	Aprx. 40 pictures per disk with index
Clip Art Sampler	£4	Illustrated index with free disk

Scanners

	Price	Type	Notes
Sharp JX-100	£640	Flatbed	16-bit colour, 200 DPI
Power scanner	£160	Hand	Mono 400 DPI
Geniscan	£130	Hand	Mono 400 DPI,105mm wide
GI Scanner	£200	Hand	Award winning b/w scanner
Sharp JX-300	£1550	Flatbed	24-bit colour, 300 DPI (A4)

Music Packages

	Price	Notes
Bars and Pipes	£170	Amazing MIDI sequencer
Dr T's Tiger Cub	£100	Nice beginners system
Sonix	NA	Oldie but a goodie — notational
Quartet	£50	Commercial 4-channel tracker
MED 3.1	Free	4 channel tracker with MIDI
OctaMED 2	£20	MED with full musical notation

Amiga Painting Systems

	Price	Notes
Deluxe Paint 4	£90	Latest — includes HAM
Photon Paint 2	£90	Powerful HAM package
Deluxe Photolab	£130	Image manipulator
Spectracolor	£70	Rival to Photon Paint?
Digi-Paint 3	£70	Power HAM-based system
My Paint	£20	Simple and cheap!
Scuplt animate series	£130+	Range of 3D packages
Draw 4D	POA	Another 3D+ system?
Turbo Silver	£145	3D rendering engine
HAM-E	£400	24-bit colour system
Vistapro	£100	Fractal landscape machine
PIXmate	£40	Advanced image processor

Titling Systems

	Price	Notes
Scala	£250	One of the best around
Broadcast Titler 2	£235	Awkward but powerful
Home Titler	£40	Basic titler
Pro Titler	£150	Powerful titling system
ZVP Video Studio	£100	Video production aids

Programming Languages

	Price	Notes
GFA BASIC	£50	Powerful applications BASIC
Blitz BASIC	£70	Fast games-tailored BASIC
AMOS BASIC	£70	Very poular and powerful BASIC
HiSoft BASIC	£50	Easy to use and popular compiler
RQ FORTH	NA	Awaiting release
Lattice C	£230	Widely used C compiler — powerful
Aztec C	£130	Popular C compiler
M2 Amiga	£125	Modula 2 — Pascal follow-up
ArgAsm	£60	The fastset 68000 assem ever
Devpac II	£60	Most widely used Amiga assem
ARexx	£50	Automating language for applications
CanDo	£130	Hypercard like -applications generator
Pascal	£3	Version of Wirth's first attempt
Smalltalk	£3	Another wierdo

Widgets

	Price	Notes
A500 dust cover	£5	Keep an A500 clean
Disk boxes	£5-£25	Price depends on storage etc
Disk drive cleaners	£3-£5	A waste of time and money!
Easyl	£270	Unique — an artist's dream digitiser
Fat Agnes	£50	For 1Mb CHIP RAM on early A500

GI Hamster	£40	Cordless mouse
Intro to Amiga	£11	VHS helper video
Monitor plinth	£25-40	Raise monitor height
Monitor switchers	£20-30	Monitor/TV sharer
Mouse house	£2	Mouse holder
Mouse mat	£3-5	Stops mouse slip
Naksha Mouse	£25	Hi-res mouse
Optical mouse	£36	A mouse without a ball!
Roboshift	£30	Auto mouse switcher
The Brush	£40	"Pen" that works like a mouse?
Tracey	£8	Budget digitiser (mouse-based)
Trackerball	£50	Mouse alternative
Truemouse	£18	Budget mouse
Virus Killers	£3	An essential buy!

D
Printer Driver Charts

Supported Printers and Print Densities

Driver	Density	Compatibility/notes
Alphacom_Alphapro_101	-	With IBM Interface
Brother_HR-15XL	-	Text only
CalComp_ColorMaster	1s	ColorMaster, Colorview 5912
CalComp_ColorMaster2	1s	As above, but the faster driver requires up to 3Mb of RAM!
Canon_PJ1080A	1s	Integrex 132/ColorJet
CBM_MPS1000	1s 2 & 5d 3 & 6t	Canon BJ-130/10e/300/330, IBM 5152 Most IBM compatibles
Diablo_630	-	Diablo 630
Diablo_Advantage_D25	-	Diablo Advantage D25
Diablo_C-150	1s	Diablo C-150
EpsonQ	1-3s 4 Mono	Epson LQ1500/2500 Star 24-10/200 Most 24-pin Epson compats.
EpsonX[CBM_MPS-1250]	1s 2 & 5d 3 & 6t	Epson EX/FX/JX/LX/MX/RX CBM MPS-1230/50/70/1550 Citizen 120D/Swift 9; Juki 5510/20; Pansonic KXP-1081, Star LC-10/10C/200 etc.
EpsonXOld	1-4,7 EP 5,6 SM	8 or 9 pin driver for use with old Epson and Star printers (Gemini 10-X for instance)

Supported Printers and Print Densities

continuedfrom page 164

Driver	Density	Compatibility/notes
Howtek Pixelmaster	1-4s	Howtek Pixelmaster
HP_DeskJet	1-4s	DeskJet and DeskJet Plus
HP_LaserJet	1-4s	LaserJet, LaserJet Plus/II DeskJet 500
HP_PaintJet	1s	HP PaintJet
HP_ThinkJet	1s	HP ThinkJet
ImagewriterII	1-4s 5-7d	Apple ImageWriter Apple ImageWriterII
Nec_Pinwriter	1-3,6s 4,5 & 7d	Nec P5/6/7/9/2200
Okidata_92	1s	Okidata 92
Okidata_293i	1 & 2s 3 & 4d	Okidata 292/293/393 Using IBM interface adaptor
Okimate_20	1s	Okimate 20
Quadram_Quadjet	-	Text only
Qume_Letterpro_20	1s	Qume LetterPro 20
Toshiba_P351C	1-2s	All Toshiba 351-C compatibles
Toshiba_P351SX	1-2s 3-4d	Toshiba 351SX, 321SL 321SLC, 341SLC
Xerox_4020	1-2	Xerox 4020

Density settings apply to graphics only.
s = Single pass printing (suitable for colour)
d = Dual pass printing (mono dumps only)
t = Three pass printing (mono dumps only)
EP = Epson mode
SM = Star mode

E
Common Questions

Q: Why do some disk icons remain on Workbench screen all the time and others come and go.

A: This is a complex one. Workbench is constantly trying to keep the desktop tidy, so as soon as a disk is no longer in use, its icon is removed from the screen. When you run a program from any disk, its icon will remain active, and on the Workbench screen, *until* the program closes down.

The same applies if you "open" a disk then remove it from the drive — while the window is open the disk icon remains on the desktop. In rare cases, a disk icon will remain even after a program has been shut down. This is caused by a bugs in the software and should never happen; it does though.

Q: My disk drives are clicking all the time. Is this normal and how can I stop them?

A: Perfectly normal. The Amiga is constantly looking at each drive to see if a disk has been inserted. Due to the drive's internal design, the Amiga has to send a "step pulse" which moves the head — first one way then the other. Some third-party external drives get around this problem with clever hardware gizmos.

The best solution is to leave the disk in the drive. You can also get a public domain program called NoClick to stop it.

Q: I've heard some A500s have a Fat Agnes — what is it and how do I know which one I have?

A: All Amiga 500s have a Fat Agnes. What you've heard about is a Fatter Agnes or Super Agnes. The original Agnes is only found in the A1000 machines. If you have a 1.3 Workbench, just open a Shell and type AVAIL. If you have a Fat Agnes the machine will show the total amount of CHIP RAM to be in excess of 1,000,000 bytes. For this to work you must have at least 1Mb RAM in the machine to start with. If not, the new Agnes won't make any noticeable difference. Super Agnes is only fitted to the A500Plus and A3000.

Q: What can I do when I get a "Task Held..." message.

A: Relax. It just means that something has gone wrong but the Amiga has caught the villain in the act. The machine is constantly running several tasks at once, so if you are still in control of yours, save your work and re-boot the machine. If you can't get control of your program this means either it, or some sub-system it relies upon, have gone down.

Q: Who or what is the Guru?

A: This is just another way of telling you something has gone seriously wrong with the software you were using. In theory, only programmers should ever see Guru meditations, in practice everyone does from time to time. By comparison, 8-bit micros and PCs just seize up; the ST displays a row of bombs and the Mac brings up a funny requester box. The information in a Guru is very valuable to a programmer. Unless you have a technical manual, you might as well ignore them unless the problem recurs with more than one package.

Q: If the Amiga has 1Mb drives why can I only get mine initialised (formatted) to 880K?

A: The drives are 1Mb, as are the disks. In practice, some of the disk's capacity is taken up by other things. The extra 120K isn't empty space, it's used as a safety margin. Some machines can only get 720K from the same equipment!

Q: The drive light on my friend's machine is amber (yellow) mine is green. What's the difference?

A: Probably none. The colour of the power and drive lights is caused by a filter which is fitted at the factory. If the green ones are out of stock, you get an amber one!

Q: What's multi-tasking?

A: Put simply, it's the process of running several programs at once with each program being unaware of the others. Every program thinks it has complete control of the machine — it's like having more than one computer in one box — and the Amiga is the only "affordable" home micro to feature it!

Q: My friend's got an STe and says it's better than the Amiga. Is he right?

A: No. There's not a lot of difference on the face of things. Each machine has its strong points — as well as weak ones. You have a great machine — be thankful for it.

Q: Why can't I use "Duplicate" from Workbench to back up my games?

A: Most games disks use a special "format" to stop people copying them and giving them away (which is illegal). Some games can be copied using Duplicate — the manual will usually tell you.

Q: My girlfriend/wife/mother thinks computers are stupid.

A: She's right! Computers are stupid — it's programs (software) that give them the semblance on sentiency. If her problem is more philosophical she's probably expressing a fear, born from a lack of understanding. Don't humour her — indulge her, give her something to do on it! Find a game she likes — one which isn't filled with moronic violence: Flimbo's Quest, Bubble Bobble, Lemmings that sort of thing.

Q: What can I do about this acne?

A: This is a computer book! What do you think I am, an agony aunt?

F
In An Emergency

If your machine breaks down, then what? Since the Amiga is so complex there are a lot of reasons why it could fail — or at least appear to. Amigas are very reliable machines and in many cases the fault lies with the setup. Here is a simple step-by-step (by no means exhaustive) guide to what to do when something seems to go wrong. All these faults are gathered from real-life experience so there's no need to feel foolish. Even experts make mistakes.

If you're still having problems after using this guide you should contact your supplier who should solve the problem on your behalf. Do not contact Commodore directly, your dealer will do that for you if necessary.

Self-Tests

When the Amiga is turned on, it goes through a series of self-tests. This is built into the ROM and helps to safeguard against trouble. What actually happens is irrelevant to the average user — unless something goes wrong!

Every time the machine is booted these tests are carried out. Watch carefully, the display goes: dark grey, light grey, then asks for a disk. On the main unit, the "Caps Lock" light flashes once (or at least it should) to indicate the keyboard is functioning correctly. If the display comes up some other colour or, rarely, the Caps Lock light flashes more than once, "there's trouble at mill!"

Don't panic. Switch off and re-check you've connected everything correctly. If you have something like an A590 or similar hanging on the expansion port of an A500 it *must* be switched on first. If not, the electronics in the machine will think something is broken and flag a serious hardware failure.

Note also, some virus killers and other resident software, announce themselves by flashing the display funny colours during boot up. This is normal and nothing to worry about. If there's a problem, screen will stay that colour. The colours mean something to Amiga engineers, they need not concern you.

Fault Chart

Fault	Possible Cause	Cure
General		
Machine won"t switch on	You haven't switched on at the mains!	Switch on. This may sound daft but if I had 1p for every call- out we'd had for this simple problem...
	The PSU is not connected to the machine	Check the lead from the PSU is firmly connected at the back of the machine. On A500 machines it fits into the small square (female) socket next to the video output. On all other machines, which have internal power supplies — there is a MALE socket on the back of the machine near a small circular grill.
	The power supply unit (PSU) is not connected at the mains.	A500 machines only: Check the PSU is plugged into the wall and the switch (if fitted) is on the ON position. If you are unsure, plug something else into the socket — a table lamp is a good test.

	The fuse is missing or faulty	Check the fuse for or try a different one. If you have bought a new plug and the fuse has blown consult a qualified electrician. DO NOT fit a 13A fuse (usually a brown case), 3A (usually a red case) is quite sufficient.
	The mains lead is wired incorrectly or has come away from the inside of the plug.	Check you have wired the plug correctly. BROWN is live, BLUE is neutral and YELLOW/GREEN striped is EARTH. These connections must be firm. Also make SURE the cord grip is secure. Better still, go for something like the MK Safety plug with the non-slip cord grip. This will help prevent future disasters.
Power light on, but no "Insert Disk" prompt	See Video	
	Dead to the world, nothing works.	Assuming you have not inserted a Workbench or some other disk. the screen should be either light grey or have a picture of a hand holding a disk. If the screen is some other colour, red, green, blue etc contact your dealer immediately to ask their advice. If you have tried to "boot" a disk, give the machine time to process it before calling the doctor. This sort of is EXTREMELY RARE.

Power		
Power light off	After switching on, the machine takes a couple of seconds to wake up and self-test the major systems.	Wait a few seconds. If the power light still does not come on, check all connections and consult advice under the general section. After the test completes the power light is switched on. Clever little beasties, these Amigas.
	When you run most music programs and other software which access the sound system, the power light goes off.	This is because the software is turning off the low-pass filter fitted to later machines to improve sound quality. Don't worry, this is quite normal.
Power light blinking	If you have a high-end machine like an Amiga 3000 which comes fitted as standard with a special processor, this problem is very common with games software.	The main cause of this is to indicate the machine is about to GURU. This Amiga term for "about to crash spectacularly with a sanguine message and frighten the living daylights out of the poor beginner" is rarely serious. The most common cause for a GURU is a fault in some software.
	Virus	Check with the software manufacturer. It may be caused by a computer virus.
	Software trickery	Some programs flash the power light to indicate disk access or other processing. It's a lazy way of saying "please wait..." This is not common practice (and discouraged by Commodore) but some people will insist on being different.

Video

No picture or picture is of poor quality.	The monitor or TV is not switched on.	Check the unit is switched on and plugged in at the mains.
	The TV lead is damaged, or not plugged in.	Damage is unlikely but you may have forgotten to plug the lead in OR plugged it into the wrong socket. The TV modulator is a separate device DO NOT plug the TV lead into the socket marked Composite Video.
	The TV is not tuned to the correct channel	If the TV has a manual tuning system — ie operated by turning a knob, try to tune the set through its full range. Some electronic tuners will lock on "ghost" signals some way from the main picture, so it may take several attempts. The picture should be crisp without any sign of "snow".
	The modulator selector switch is in the wrong position	Consult the manual supplied with your machine and move the channel selector switch to the other position.
	The monitor lead is loose	This typically shows up when the picture suddenly goes green or red. Ensure the monitor leads are plugged in firmly at both ends. Do NOT lift the machine up at the front since this can dislodge the lead.
	The monitor lead is not suitable	This may affect some Sony TV sets with separate SCART inputs to accept satellite broadcasts and direct feed video. Check with the supplier who sold you the lead.

	The input selector switch is in the wrong position	This is a common problem with many monitors and some combined TV/monitors. Check with the manufacturer's manual to find out if a separate "input selector" switch is fitted and try the other position. Some TV/monitors do this automatically when they sense a signal on the input.
	The modulator is damaged	This may happen if you plug in or remove the modulator when the machine is switched on. NEVER do this. If you suspect the modulator is faulty get it checked by your dealer.
Some of the picture is missing	The Preferences setting for video position is incorrect	Boot your Workbench disk and start the Preferences program. Move the pointer over the white box at the centre of the blue panel. Press and hold the left mouse button. Now move the mouse until the screen is centred. Release the left mouse button and click on the SAVE button. This may apply to any programs which have to be started from their own Workbench.
	The monitor or TV's vertical/horizontal position adjustments are wrong	If the adjustment is external you can try to alter them. Otherwise refer the problem to qualified personnel.
Picture is shaky	The application is running in "interlaced" mode	This is quite normal and can be fixed with a flicker fixer; an expensive solution though.
	Your monitor's horizontal/vertical sync is out of adjustment	This should not happen unless you have been tinkering or the monitor is faulty. Some of these adjustments are inside the case — get a TV engineer to check this for you.
	Your power supply or another TV is interfering with the set.	This can happen when two PSUs are placed close together and/or near a monitor. Try moving the supplies around and see what difference it makes.

Audio		
No sound	Volume is turned down or a muting device is operating.	Increase the volume on your monitor or switch the mute off.
	You have connected the external sound to the wrong input.	At the hi-fi end plug the leads into the spare sockets marked AUX or Auxiliary. If you have done this, make sure the selector switch is pointing at the correct input. If the auxiliary input is in use you may be able to use the tape monitor, CD or tuner input. Do not use the sockets for record player. This is also common on the 1084S monitor where the audio and video inputs are grouped together.
	On hi-fi systems is the lead connected to the correct input and is the correct input selected with the source selector?	If you want to connect to a hi-fi system, you will have to buy a separate lead — usually 2 x phono male --> 2 x phono male.
	On TV-based systems the Y adaptor may not be plugged in correctly	Check the Y adaptor is fitted correctly.
	On monitor-based systems, sound is usually routed via a separate lead or bridged from the SCART (video) connector.	Check the sound tap is wired correctly.
Poor sound quality	On TV-based systems only, sound is affected by the tuning.	Check as for poor or no picture
One channel "missing"	Check as for No Sound	

Disk		
Noisy	Noisy disks are a fact of life. You'll have to live with this one. If the sound is more like a metallic scraping, it may be the disk shutter has become jammed.	Remove the disk and try again.
Won't load games	This can be anything from a faulty disk drive to a virus.	Read through the rest of this section and if all else fails take the problem disk to your dealer.

Mouse/Joystick		
Mouse/ Joystick not working at all	Mouse/joystick not plugged in	Plug it in! The plugs can work loose if the machine is lifted from the front. (NEVER tilt the machine from the front.)
Right mouse button won't activate any menus	Intuition has tied the menu to another window — probably a CLI window in this case.	Click inside the main screen — such as the Workbench screen.
One or both buttons not working	Microswitch jiggered	Get the unit checked by a professional. This problem is endemic with low-cost joysticks, the only solution is to buy a better one.
	Lead faulty	Test the mouse on another machine
"Jittery" or "jerky" operation	The mouse rollers are dirty	This is a fact of life but it can be very disturbing when it first happens. As the ball moves over a surface it picks up a minute amount of dirt which it deposits on the rollers. After a while the dirt gets so thick it starts to foul the ball. In very severe cases the ball can jam completely.
	The mouse is in the joystick socket and vice-versa	Swap the two units over! This is a surprisingly common mistake and an easy one to make.

Keyboard		
No keys working at all	This is a very common and often disturbing problem for the beginner — even experts find it a nuisance. In most cases this is caused by Intuition switching off the active window and the windows title bar will be shadowed — made feint.	Click (press the left mouse button) inside the window you wish to type into.
	The window you were working in has been de-activated by you selecting another screen.	See above
	The window you were working in has been de-activated by Intuition opening another window in this screen or some other screen. This can happen if Intuition needs your urgent attention (to insert a disk) by bringing up a so-called requester box.	This can come as a bit of a shock at first. If you can still see the window you want to work in click (press the left mouse button) somewhere within its boundaries. In some cases however, a program (say, Deluxe Paint) will bring up its own screen and Intuition will bring the Workbench screen back temporarily. Here, you must press the right "Amiga" key and "M" at the same time to push Workbench out of the way. In very severe cases you may need to use the depth gadgets to find your screen. When your screen is at the front you will still have to click inside it to make it accept input from you.
	The window you were working in has been de-activated by a program such as SunWindows or Autopoint.	If this has happened, just move the mouse over the window you want to work in and keep it there. This is a very common mistake when such programs are active — if you don't understand them, don't use them.

Some keys in the wrong places	Happens with all software	This can happen when your Workbench has not been configured correctly. As shipped by Commodore, some Workbenches have the wrong "keyboard map" set up.
	Happens with some software	If this is the case, your software is at fault and the only recourse is to get it changed for a version which reads the keyboard correctly. There is no real excuse for this sort of bug; but you may have to live with it.
One or more keys not working	Wrong keymap loaded	See above

Printer

Nothing prints	The printer is not switched on	Switch the printer on. If this is the first time you have used the machine get it to do a self-test also. This varies from machine to machine but usually means holding down either "Form Feed (FF)" or "Line Feed (LF)" while switching on. Consult the manual before trying this.
	Printer is not "on-line"	Press the button marked "on-line" or switch on and off again.
	Printer is out of paper	Insert some paper — sounds obvious, but people forget this basic necessity!
	The printer is not plugged into the computer	Check all leads and cabling from the computer to the printer and the mains cable. If you have forgotten to plug the computer to printer cable in at one end SWITCH EVERYTHING OFF FIRST!
	The printer interface has not been selected from Preferences	Run the "Preferences" tool and select the appropriate type of printer interface to suit your machine. In most cases this will be parallel — which is default. If you have a serial printer you'll also need to set the baud rate and parity etc. The exact settings vary from machine to machine, so you will have to check with the printer's manual or your supplier.
Won't print text	The printer ribbon has become dislodged from the print head or is not fitted.	Ensure you have fitted the ribbon (or ink cartridge) correctly.

	Wrong printer driver installed or no printer driver present	Copy the correct printer driver for your machine to the Workbench disk and select it from Preferences.
Won't print graphics	You are trying to print graph ics on a daisy wheel or other text only printer	This can be done — but it's VERY complex. At this stage do not attempt to print any graphics until you under stand the machine. Better still, get a proper graphics printer.
Poor graphics	Preferences settings are not suitable	See the relevant section elsewhere in this book
	You are trying to print colour graphics text on a mono printer	Change the colour of the text — see the manual with your word processor. If you are using Notepad, you may be able to improve the situation by altering the "Preferences" settings.
Poor text	Ribbon is badly worn or ink cartridge needs replacement	Replace the ribbon or ink cartridge.

Glossary

680x0: Sometimes used to refer to any model in Motorola's 68000 family of microprocessors. Currently there are five in the range: 68000; 68010; 68020; 68030 and 68040 – each increasing in speed and power.

68000: Base processor used in most Amigas. Other processors are available and range from 68010 — which isn't much different, to the 68040 which is a wolf in a pure new wool. See also: CPU

A500: The most basic Amiga still in production and the only one ever to have an integral keyboard and base unit.

A501: Commodore's 512K RAM expansion and battery backed-up clock for the A500. See also: A500

A590: Commodore's hard disk drive for the A500. See also: HD, A501

A690: Commoodore's CD drive for the A500 which supposedly makes it CDTV compatible. Time will tell.

A1000: The original Amiga. Comes standard with precious little RAM and Kickstart on disk.

A2000: An A1000 in a different case with better expansion — produced by Commodore Germany and no longer in production.

A3000/3500: The latest in Amiga systems. All singing — all dancing, but still can't make tea. Comes with the latest version of Workbench.

AmigaDOS: Amiga Disk Operating System. Commodore's multi-tasking DOS. See also: DOS, Kickstart

APL: A Programming Language. Honest, that's what it means

Assignment: The logical (DOS) name representing a device, directory or path. A kind of shorthand. Users can (in theory) read and write assignments just as the would read and write devices — without having to know what is behind it. See also: Device, Path

Asynchronous: A child process which once started, runs independently of the process which started it. See also: Synchronous

B2000: The "real" Amiga 2000 and till recently the flagship of the fleet. Aimed at professional users with internal expansion slots. Features 1Mb RAM and separate keyboard/base unit as standard.

BASIC: Beginners All-purpose Symbolic Instruction Code. A universal programming language for all men. Great if you get a good one — bad if you don't.

Baud: Approximately, bits-per-second. A guide to the speed achieveable for a serial device such as a modem.

Bit: A single binary value — either one or zero. When quoting memory size, some manufacturers quote xxxxx Mbits — the number of Kbytes multiplied by eight.

Blitter: Block Image Transfer [unit]. A piece of custom-built hardware designed to support graphics displays. It copies "rectangular" blocks of memory at phenomenal rates and because screen displays are just windows on memory, the blitter can be used to manipulate graphics and even control disk drives. On the Amiga, the blitter (also called a blimmer or block image manipulator) has been incorporated into the Fat Agnes chip.

BOB: Blitter Object. A type of sprite (moveable screen image) controlled by the blitter. Unlike true sprites, BOBs directly affect screen memory. Also, although slower than sprites, BOBs are not limited to size and number of colours.

Boolean: Rarely seen in AmigaDOS (at command level). This term is used to indicate a result being returned is either TRUE or FALSE.

Boot or Bootstrap: The process of starting the machine or a piece of software, viz: "First boot your Workbench disk, then boot FootBall by double clicking on its icon." The term boot derives from a famous expressionism about "pulling yourself up by your own bootstraps [laces]." Hence also the name, Kickstart. Although this term has been adopted by computer users, its roots are in electronics and the analogy of booting isn't accurate. Unless you think of it as giving the machine a good kick to wake it up.

Byte: A unit of measurement in the computer binary system. A byte is a standard unit of store and consists of eight bits or two nybbles.

C: A programming language used to develop operating systems like Kickstart and AmigaDOS. Also used for a bundle of other things because it's the in thing to do.

CDTV: Commodore Dynamic Total Vision: The latest development in the Amiga 500 systems. An A500 with a super high-quality CD attached.

Centronics port: Generic term for the printer port.

Charityware: Shareware software used and distributed in the same way, but instead of paying the authors for its use, you are expected to make a contribution to charity.

Child: See sibling

CHIP RAM: Memory shared between the custom chips and the CPU. On machines fitted with FAST RAM, this memory is usually only used for the display and sound samples. Because of the way the Amiga works, several *displays* can live in CHIP at once – even if they're hidden behind others and this can often lead to confusing and unexpected "out of memory" errors.

Click: The action of positioning the mouse pointer over and icon (or any other object come to that) and pressing the left mouse button once.

Co Processor: See FPU

Cold boot: To reset the machine by switching it off and and then on again. The machine must be left OFF for at least 10 seconds before switching on or the sensitive chips may sustain expensive damage.

CPU: Central Processing Unit. This is where all the hard work gets done — the machine's brain if you like. The Amiga uses the 680x0 series of CPUs with the 68000 being the most common. The 68010 is sometimes offered as a cheap upgrade.

Daemon: Variant spelling of Demon. Crops up in AmigaDOS 2 when referring to the new preferences managers.

Daughterboard: A sub PCB supplied with some items of hardware which is "piggy-backed" into one or more IC sockets on the motherboard. Daughterboards are often used to overcome design problems in certain types of hardware such as large RAM expansions and processor accelerators.

Device name: The name given to any device. The name is arbitrary but MUST be followed by a colon — DH0:, DF0:, JH0:, CON:, SPEAK: etc.

Device: A hardware device (such as a floppy disk) used by the Amiga OR a logical device driven by, or simulated in, software. See also: Logical Device

Directory: A group of objects stored on a disk OR the place on the disk where those objects are stored. If a disk was a filing cabinet, the directories are drawers in the cabinet. See also: Object

Disk: Generic term for small electromagnetic devices used to store programs and information. Read from and written to by disk drives.

DMA: Direct Memory Access. A technique whereby data is written to, or retrieved from RAM directly instead of having to go via the CPU. DMA usually occurs when the processor is *asleep* so to speak – while it is processing program instructions. This makes the process both transparent and very fast.

DOS: Device (or disk) operating system. The part of a computer system which controls all the external hardware devices such as disk drives, printers and so on. See Device

Double-click: The action of positioning the mouse pointer over an icon and pressing the left mouse button twice in quick succession.

DPaint: Common contraction for Deluxe Paint, Electronic Art's standard Amiga paint package beloved of many Amiga artists. So good it's been converted to other machines too.

Drag: Moving an icon or icons by selecting them and then moving the mouse without releasing the left button.

DTP: Desktop Publishing. The use of computers to replace conventional systems of typesetting and paste up. DTP is more convenient, faster, less prone to error and cheaper.

ECS: Enhanced Chip Set. An often misused term that is used to collectively describe the recently upgraded versions of the Amiga's custom chips, Agnes and Denise.

EXEC: The multi-tasking executive. The part of Kickstart controlling all the low-level resource and memory management and the tasks. See also: Kickstart

Extra Half-brite: 64 colour screen mode simulated in hardware. In this mode you have 32 colours — plus another 32 of half the intensity.

FAST RAM: Random access memory which the custom chips have no access to. Although the CPU can run programs slightly faster if they are located here because the RAM access isn't being shared. The actual difference can usually only be measured in tens of micro seconds – so slight it's transparent.

FFS: Fast Filing System. A new version of the DOS filing system developed for hard drives initially but now available on floppy for the Workbench 2-based machines. Although slightly less reliable than OFS (the original system), FFS is much faster and gives around five percent improvement in storage capacity per formatted device.

FIFO: First In First Out. A pipeline buffer — data is inserted at one end of the buffer and read out from the other end in the same order. If the sequence 12345 written to a LIFO buffer, would be read back 54321. See also: LIFO, Pipe

File: Anything saved on a disk for later retrieval — except directories. Files can be created by users or the system. The Workbench (system disk) contains many files. See also: Object

Firmware: Software held in ROM. See also: ROM

FORTH: A programming language devised to control radio telescopes.

FPU: Floating Point Unit. A very clever piece of hardware which can perform floating point computations at incredible speed. Rivalling the CPU in complexity, these little beasties can speed maths intensive programs by as much as 500 or 600%

Fractal: Term used to describe a special mathematical formulae which seems to have an infinite number of possibilities. Benoit Mandlebrot — who first described the phenomena, also gives his name to the most commonly seen interpretation — the Mandlebrot Set.

Frame Grabber: Something like a Genlock, only this one grabs "frames" from the video signal and stores them in memory for later processing and retrieval.

G or Gb: Like K this means Giga. 1Gb is about 1 million, million bytes or about 1,000,000,000,000.

Gadget: An Intuition managed object. It could be a button, an icon or a sliding knob — Intuition doesn't mind. The title bar on most Intuition windows doubles a drag gadget.

Genlock: A special device for mixing a video signal, say from a video camera or recorder, with the screen display generated by the Amiga. The video signal shows through the "black" parts of the Amiga display. This is akin to blue screening on TV.

GUI: Graphical User Interface#(see GUI). Any operating system which uses graphics to help the user find their way around the disk operating system. The first (and still probably the best) is Finder on the Apple Macintosh. Other examples are Windows, X-Windows and GEM. The Amiga's GUI is called Workbench. See also: Workbench

Hacker: A computer expert — of late a term plagiarised by pirates who also consider themselves experts.

HAM: Hold and Modify. Special screen mode used by the Amiga to display 4096 colours at once — yet using only a fraction of the amount of memory required by normal methods.

Handles: I/O ports where processes can gather and output information. C programmers should already know these as STDIN, STDOUT and STDERR.

Hard Disk Drive or HDD. Just like a floppy disk drive only MUCH bigger. Amiga hard disk drives start with a standard storage capacity of 20Mb and rise to over 300Mb! Hard disks are like Porches; expensive, fragile and very fast. See also: Device

Hardware: The electronics making up a computer system or part of it. See also: Software, Firmware.

Icon: Small picture used as a memory aid in WIMP systems. See also: WIMP, GUI

IDE: Integrated Drive Electronics. Controller system used in hard drives – more common on the PC than the Amiga though. See SCSI.

IFF: Interchange File Format. This was a co-invention of Electronic Arts and Commodore Amiga Inc. It programs to exchange data very easily and avoids the situation on say, the PC, where dozens of graphics packages each save data in a different way. The IFF format covers graphics and animation, sound and music, even formatted text has been adopted recently.

Intuition: The core of the Amiga's WIMP system. See also: WIMP

K or Kb: Generic terms for Kilo adopted by the computer industry. 1K = 1024 units; 1Kb =

1024 bytes. The actual number is derived in the binary system as 2^8 =1024.

Kickstart: The Amiga's Operating System (OS). Contained on a ROM — or in WOM on A1000s and very early A3000s. Kickstart is what makes the machine tick. It contains most of the software that make the Amiga work. See also: ROM, Firmware

Library: A series of shared routines with a common goal. Libraries come in many flavours — the dos.library looks after the DOS routines, the graphics.library oversees graphics and text printing, the icon.library manages the Workbench and the branch.library lends books. See also: Shared, ROM

Licenceware: Shareware software distributed by licensed vendors. The software is subject to copyright, and the vendor charges an extra fee which is passed directly to the authors.

LIFO: Last In First Out. A stack buffer — each new item of data is inserted on top of the existing data. When something tries to read from a LIFO it always receives the newest data. If the sequence 12345 written to a LIFO buffer, would be read back 12345. See also: FIFO

List: EXEC term used to describe a series of items all joined together in memory. Each item in the list is called a NODE. Most Amiga lists are doubly-linked structures where each child points to both its ancestor and its sibling.

Lists are very important in Amiga programming but not relevant to user level AmigaDOS. See also: EXEC

Logical device: A hardware device simulated in software. See also: Assignment

Longword or Lunch: Four bytes or 32 bits. A standard unit of measurement of computer memory for 16/32 CPUs.

M or Mb or Megabyte: Unit of measurement equal to approximately one million bytes. The actual number is derived in the binary system as 2^16 or 1048576.

Menu bar: List of menu titles accessed by pressing the right mouse button. See also: WIMP, Intuition

Menu: List of items/choices. See also: Menu Bar

MFLOPS: Millions of Floating Points calculations per Second. A standard speed figure quoted for many modern processors and accelerator cards.

Micon: A moving or animated icon. Not very common on the Amiga — the best examples are animated mouse pointers like Animouse and Sleepy. Kickstart 2 uses a front-end micon to tell you it wants a disk. See also: Icon

MIDI: Musical Instrument Digital Interface. A simple standard devised to connect all manner of keyboard and musical synthesizers together and control them remotely – either by computer or by each other.

MIPS: Million Instructions per Second. A standard speed figure showing raw speed comparisons. By their nature, MFLOPS give a more accurate representation for number-crunching applications.

MMU: Memory Management Unit. Part of the 68040 CPU – takes care of everything to do with the memory.

Modula II: A programming language and what Pascal should have been all along.

Modulator: Device used to connect the Amiga to a domestic television set.

Monitor: The display.

Motherboard: The main PCB containing all the discrete components and ICs that make a computer operate.

Mouse: Small odiferous rodent. Also small unit used to move the pointer in a WIMP system.

NTSC: National Television Standards Committee. TV standard used mainly in the US and Canada. Features 200 or 400 lines at 60Hz refresh rate whereas PAL has 256 or 512 lines and a 50Hz refresh. Defined in *Confessions of a Computer Journalist* as Never The Same Colour, because of the atrocious colour rendition when NTSC broadcasts are converted to PAL.

Nybble: Half a byte or four bits. See Byte, Bit

Object: In AmigaDOS an object is USUALLY a file or another directory but it can be a device or assignment. Workbench objects are icons. See also: File

Orphan (process): Sibling processes can be orphaned if the parent process shuts down – this should never happen.

Orphan directory: A sibling directory which has lost its parent. This only happens when the disk structure is corrupted and can sometimes be recovered using DiskDoctor.

OS: Operating System. See also: Kickstart

Overscan: Special screen mode used by the Amiga where the picture has no visible borders — that is, it fills the entire monitor screen.

PAL/SECAM: TV system in use in the UK and Europe. Gives 256 or 512 lines on a full screen. See also: NTSC

Palette: Part of the hardware where colours are mixed to achieve the end result. The Amiga has a 4096 colour palette which means you have a choice of 4096 colours, shades and intensities. Few artists use more than 20 or 30 shades in a [computer] painting but the effects can be startling.

Parallel port: Yet another name for the printer port.

Parent Directory: The directory level one level higher than the current directory.

Parent Process: The process which started a sub-process (sibling or child process).

Pascal: Computer language named after a great philosopher who would turn in his grave if he knew about it.

Path: The position in the directory tree which points to an object or group of objects — a pathway or road. See also: Directory

PD: Public Domain. Software which has been placed in the public domain by its author can be freely copied by anyone. It is however, still copyright and subject to the copyright laws. If it doesn't say Public Domain on it, it isn't.

Peripheral: External device — such as a disk drive or printer which the computer system does not NEED to operate. Monitors are sometimes mistakenly called peripherals since they have to be purchased separately. An Amiga without a monitor is like a car with no wheels. See also: Device

Pipe: An AmigaDOS pipe is a small FIFO buffer based in RAM. Any process can write data to the pipe in the same way it could write to a disk. However pipes become FULL very quickly, so the receiving process must read from the pipe at the same time as the sending process is filling it. Unlike disks, a process may attempt to read from a pipe even when it's empty — without causing an error, it just has to wait until something enters the pipe. Similarly, when the pipe is filled, the writing process is made to wait until some data is read from it. See also: FIFO, LIFO

Pointer or pointing device: An arrowhead [or some similar design] moved by the mouse (usually) to "point" at the icon they wish to work on. See also: Icon, Micon

Port: Usually an external socket where other expansion is added. The sockets for mouse, joystick, disk drive, printer, and so on are all ports. This term is also used in multi-tasking but that's all programming stuff (bleah).

Process: These are just high-level tasks maintained by AmigaDOS. Unlike tasks, processes can access the dos.library and perform disk access. There is an upper limit of 20 processes running at once prior to AmigaDOS 2. Exceeding this limit gives the confusing error: Task table full — in fact the process table is full, tasks are managed in a list. See also: List, Task

Project: Workbench term for a file created by a Workbench Tool. Projects can be anything from sound samples to pictures.

PAD: Paula, Agnes, Denise. The three main custom chips which afford the Amiga its personality.

PSU: Power Supply Unit. A mains power adaptor supplied with larger external hardware to avoid taking the Amiga A500's existing unit.

RAM: Random Access Memory. Programs and data are temporarily stored here whilst the machine is switched on. When power is removed, the contents of RAM are lost. See also: ROM

Read only: Applied to files or disks this means the object cannot be written to. When applied to disks, it also means the disk cannot be formatted.

Requester box: These are used when a program or the machine either, needs confirmation from you, or, needs information from you. Requesters can be simple: "Please insert Volume Workbench1.3 in any drive" or devilishly complex with dozens of values to enter. All requesters have (or should have) one thing in common: a confirmation button and a cancel button. The text used can be variable, but usually it'll be along the lines of "OK" or "YES" and "Cancel" or "Ooops, forget it!"

ROM: Read Only Memory. Just like RAM, only permanent. ROMs are used to hold the programs which make the machine behave like a computer. See Firmware, Kickstart.

Root directory: The first directory on any disk. All other sibling directories link back to this one.

RS232: Another name for the serial port.

SCART: Standard connector on many monitors and even some domestic TVs. The Amiga can be connected directly to this with the correct lead.

Screen: The area where windows are displayed. On the Amiga many screens can make up the display — each one having its own bitmap.

Screens — like windows — can be depth arranged and pulled down to reveal others. See Window. See also: Device

SCSI: Small Computer Systems Interface. Pronounced *Skuzzy*, this has become the standard interface for most Amiga hard disks and other mass-storage peripherals. This is a techie term you'll see mentioned, but few users need to bother what it all means. See Disk drive

Shared routine: A small program written so that many programs can execute it at the same time. Shared routines are the backbone of resident code, all the Amiga libraries are central to multi-tasking. See also: Library

Shareware: Software which has been placed in the public domain by its author for the purposes of demonstration. Most Shareware titles are complete and fully working, however you are expected to pay a registration fee to the author if you intend to use it on a regular basis. The actual licence varies from package to package.

Shell/CLI: Typically an interface to DOS where the user has to enter instructions by hand. This is much more complex than using a GUI but also more powerful.

Sibling (directory): A directory contained within a directory. All siblings must have a parent – which can be the root directory or some other sibling. They may also contain their own children.

Sibling (process): A process which has been created (spawned) by another process and has inherited its handles.

Sibling: A child — usually refers to processes and tasks. Also applied (rarely) to directories. See also: Directory, Process

SIMM/SIPPS: Special type of RAM package used in the latest Amiga systems.

SIMMS: Simultaneous In-line Memory Modules. Pre-built RAM upgrades that although more expensive than conventional "beetles", are far easier to fit.

Software: Programs used to drive the hardware. See also: Hardware, Firmware

Sprite: A small screen object generated by the display hardware. Sprites are "ghost" images generated as part of the display and never affect display memory – a side effect of this means they are generated at blinding speed. More limited than BOBs, sprites can be the height of the screen, but a maximum of 16 pixels wide.

Synchronous process: A child process which forces the parent process to wait until it completes. See also: Asynchronous

Task: A low-level program controlled by EXEC. Tasks are the backbone of the Amiga controlling everything from the keyboard to the disk drives. Tasks can do almost anything — but they are not allowed to open the dos.library. There is no limit to the number of tasks running under EXEC apart from memory and speed restrictions. See also: Process

Thru Port: Socket at the rear of external disk drives (for instance) which allows the addition of more drives in a chain. The standard Amiga A500 can only support one external drive unless you invest in a more powerful power supply.

Tool: Workbench terminology for a program or software application.

Trapdoor: Small flap underneath current A500 models where the A501 and other proprietary RAM expansion modules are fitted.

Trashcan: Special area of a Workbench disk where icons can be moved temporarily. These icons and their associated tools can be deleted by activating "Empty Trash" from the Workbench. Icons remain in the trashcan until you remove them or empty the can.

UNIX: Alternative, multi-user operating system from AT & T. Very fast, very powerful and industry standard.

Vanilla: This is sometimes used to refer to an unexpanded machine — as it is supplied by Commodore. A vanilla A500 for instance, has

512K of RAM and a single disk drive. It's also a very nice flavour of ice cream.

VDU: Visual Display Unit. See Monitor.

Virus: Rogue program which is introduced into the system by person or persons unknown. The best way to catch one is to use pirated software or PD software from a dubious source.

Volume: A disk or a disk's name.

Vulcan nerve death grip: The act of pressing CTRL Left-Amiga Right- Amiga at the same time.

Warm boot: To reset the machine using a Vulcan nerve death grip. This clears all memory and resets the machine back to its initial configuration. Some software — like viruses — will survive this sort of boot.

WIMP: Windows, Icons, Menus and Pointers. Windows, Icons, Mice and Pull-down menus. There are several generic interpretations of this acronym, of which, this seems the most popular. Used to describe a "simple user interface" to DOS first envisaged by Rank Xerox. See also: DOS, GUI, Workbench

Window: Part of the screen partitioned off from the rest where programs can display information as text or graphics. The concept is similar to the screens found on older machines like the BBC Micro or the Spectrum. On the Amiga though, every program thinks it has total control of the window — this is the essence of a good

WIMP environment. Windows are just part of the display and are attached to a screen. See also: Screen

WOM: Write Once Memory. This only applies to the Amiga A1000 (a very early machine) and later development models — which are supplied with Kickstart on disk. When the machine is first switched on, Kickstart is loaded from disk into this 256k area of RAM. Once loaded, the RAM behaves exactly like ROM — hence WOM. See Kickstart.

Word or Snack: Two bytes or 16 bits. A standard unit of measurement in larger computer systems like the Amiga.

Workbench: The Amiga's WIMP ended DOS environment or GUI. This is the area where you will do most of your work until you feel more secure with the machine. See also: DOS, GUI, WIMP, Mouse.

Index

A

B

C

R

S